MW01278052

NORTH KOREAN FOREIGN RELATIONS IN THE POST–COLD WAR WORLD

Samuel S. Kim

April 2007

*****

The views expressed in this report are those of the author and do not necessarily reflect the official policy or position of the Department of the Army, the Department of Defense, or the U.S. Government. This report is cleared for public release; distribution is unlimited.

*****

Research for this monograph was completed in October 2006.

*****

Comments pertaining to this report are invited and should be forwarded to: Director, Strategic Studies Institute, U.S. Army War College, 122 Forbes Ave, Carlisle, PA 17013-5244.

*****

All Strategic Studies Institute (SSI) publications are available on the SSI homepage for electronic dissemination. Hard copies of this report also may be ordered from our homepage. SSI's homepage address is: *www.StrategicStudiesInstitute.army.mil.*

*****

The Strategic Studies Institute publishes a monthly e-mail newsletter to update the national security community on the research of our analysts, recent and forthcoming publications, and upcoming conferences sponsored by the Institute. Each newsletter also provides a strategic commentary by one of our research analysts. If you are interested in receiving this newsletter, please subscribe on our homepage at *www.StrategicStudiesInstitute.army. mil/newsletter/.*

ISBN 1-58487-290-X

FOREWORD

North Korea's foreign relations are a blend of contradiction and complexity. They start from the incongruity between Pyongyang's highly touted policy of *juche*, or self-reliance, and North Korea's extended and heavy reliance on foreign aid and assistance over the 6 decades of its existence. This aid—both military and economic—in the first 4 decades came from China, the Soviet Union, and communist bloc states; in the past 2 decades, this aid has come from countries including China, South Korea, and the United States.

In this monograph, Dr. Samuel Kim examines North Korea's foreign relations with China, Russia, Japan, the United States, and South Korea during the post-Cold War era. He argues that central to understanding North Korea's international behavior in the 21st century is the extent to which the policies of the United States have shaped that behavior. Although some readers may not agree with all of Dr. Kim's interpretations and assessments, they nevertheless will find his analysis simulating and extremely informative.

This publication is the fifth in a series titled "Demystifying North Korea," the products of a project directed by Dr. Andrew Scobell. The first monograph, *North Korea's Strategic Intentions*, written Dr. Scobell, was published in July 2005. The second monograph, *Kim Jong Il and North Korea: The Leader and the System*, also written by Dr. Scobell, appeared in March 2006. The third monograph, *North Korean Civil-Military Trends: Military-First Politics to a Point*, written by Mr. Ken Gause, appeared in October 2006. The fourth monograph, *North Korea's Military Conventional and Unconventional Military Capabilities and Intentions* (forthcoming March

2007), was written by Captain John Sanford (USN) and Dr. Scobell. Future monographs will examine North Korea's economy and assess future scenarios. The Strategic Studies Institute is pleased to make this monograph publicly available.

DOUGLAS C. LOVELACE, JR.
Director
Strategic Studies Institute

BIOGRAPHICAL SKETCH OF THE AUTHOR

SAMUEL S. KIM is an adjunct professor of political science and senior research scholar at the Weatherhead East Asian Institute, Columbia University, New York. He previously taught at the Foreign Affairs Institute, Beijing, China, as a Fulbright professor (1985–86); and at the Woodrow Wilson School of Public and International Affairs, Princeton University, Princeton, New Jersey (1986–93). Dr. Kim is the author or editor of 22 books on East Asian international relations and world order studies, including his most recent publications, *The International Relations of Northeast Asia* (editor; Rowman & Littlefield, 2004) and *The Two Koreas and the Great Powers* (Cambridge University Press, 2006). He has published more than 150 articles in edited volumes and leading international relations journals, including *American Journal of International Law, International Interactions, International Organization, Journal of Peace Research, World Politics, World Policy Journal; Asian Survey; Asian Perspective; China Quarterly;* and *Journal of East Asian Studies.* Dr. Kim holds an M.I.A. and Ph.D. from Columbia University.

SUMMARY

Any attempt to understand North Korean foreign relations in the post–Cold War world is to be confronted with a genuine puzzle of both real-world and theoretical significance. On the one hand, in the post–Cold War era North Korea — officially known as the Democratic People's Republic of Korea (DPRK) — has been seen by many as a failed state on the verge of explosion or implosion. On the other hand, not only has North Korea survived, despite a rapid succession of external shocks — the crumbling of the Berlin Wall, the end of both the Cold War and superpower rivalry, and the demise of the Soviet Union — all on top of a series of seemingly fatal internal woes, including spreading famine, deepening socialist alienation, and the death of its founder, the "eternal president" Kim Il Sung. But with its nuclear and missile brinkmanship diplomacy, it has become a focus of regional and global prime-time coverage.

Paradoxically, Pyongyang seems to have turned its weakness into strength by playing its "collapse card," driving home the point that it is anything but a Fourth World banana republic that would disappear quietly without a big fight or a huge mess, a mess that no outside neighboring power would be willing or able to clean up. In fact, not only has North Korea, the weakest of the six main actors in the region, continued to exist, but it has also catapulted itself to the position of primary driver of Northeast Asian geopolitics through its strategic use of nuclear brinkmanship diplomacy. From this transformed geopolitical landscape emerges the greatest irony of the region: today, in the post–Cold War world, North Korea seems to have a more secure sovereignty itself, while posing greater security risks to its neighbors, than has ever been the case in recent history.

The starting premise of this monograph is that for all the uniqueness of the regime and its putative political autonomy, post–Kim Il Sung North Korea has been subject to the same external pressures and dynamics that are inherent in an increasingly interdependent and interactive world. The foreign relations that define the place of North Korea in the international community today are the result of the trajectories that Pyongyang has chosen to take—or was forced to take—given its national interests and politics. In addition, the choices of the North Korean state are constrained by the international environment in which they interact, given its location at the center of Northeast Asian geopolitics in which the interests of the Big Four (China, Russia, Japan, and the United States) inevitably compete, clash, mesh, coincide, etc., as those nations pursue their course in the region. North Korea per se is seldom of great importance to any of the Big Four, but its significance is closely tied to and shaped by the overall foreign policy goals of each of the Big Four Plus One (South Korea). Thus North Korea is seen merely as part of the problem or part of the solution for Northeast Asia.

On the basis of historical and comparative analysis of the conduct of North Korean foreign policy, especially the turbulent relations with the Big Four plus the relationship with South Korea, the main objective here is to track, explain, and assess North Korea's foreign policy behavior in the post–Cold War and post–Kim Il Sung era, using a behavior-centered approach. What is most striking about post–Cold War North Korean foreign policy is not the centrality of the Big Four but rather the extent to which the United States has figured in the major changes and shifts in Pyongyang's international behavior. North Korea has sought and found a new troika of life-supporting geopolitical patrons in China, South Korea, and Russia, and also a new pair of life-supporting geo-economic patrons in China and South Korea, even as America's dominant perception of North Korea has shifted significantly from that of a poor nation in need of a life-support system to that of an aggressive nation representing a mortal threat. As if in fear of the DPRK's "tyranny of proximity," however, all three of North Korea's contiguous neighbors — China, Russia, and South Korea — have tended to be reluctant to support Washington's hard-line strategy.

Although the future of North Korea is never clear, the way the outside world — especially the Big Four plus Seoul — responds to Pyongyang is closely keyed to the way North Korea responds to the outside world. North Korea's future is malleable rather than rigidly predetermined. This nondeterministic image of the future of the post–Kim Il Sung system opens up room for the outside world to use whatever leverage it might have to nudge North Korean leaders toward opting for a particular future scenario over another less benign in the coming years.

NORTH KOREAN FOREIGN RELATIONS IN THE POST–COLD WAR WORLD

INTRODUCTION

To understand North Korean foreign relations in the post–Cold War world is to be confronted with a genuine puzzle of both real-world . On the one hand, in the post–Cold War era North Korea—officially known as the Democratic People's Republic of Korea (DPRK)—has been seen by many as a failed state on the verge of explosion or implosion. This dire assessment stems from the troublesome fact that the country has encountered a rapid succession of external shocks—the crumbling of the Berlin Wall, the end of both the Cold War and superpower rivalry, the demise of the Soviet Union and international communism, Moscow-Seoul normalization, and Beijing-Seoul normalization—on top of a series of internal woes, including the death of its founder, the "eternal president" Kim Il Sung, a downward spiral of industrial output, food/energy/hard currency shortages, shrinking trade, and deepening systemic dissonance, with the resulting famine killing at least 3–5 percent of the population in the latter half of the 1990s.

Thus for the first time since the Korean War, the question of the future of North Korea—whether it will survive or collapse, slowly or suddenly—has prompted a flurry of debates and has provoked many on-the-fly pundits and soothsayers of one kind or another in the United States. Many of these predicted that in the wake of Kim Il Sung's death, the DPRK would collapse within 6 months; or that in less than 3 years, Korea would have a German-style reunification by absorption.

1

The popularity of this "collapsist" scenario also has been evident in the policy communities of some of the neighboring states. In 1994 and 1995, for example, South Korean President Kim Young Sam jumped on the collapsist bandwagon when he depicted North Korea as a "broken airplane" headed for a crash landing that would be followed by a quick Korean reunification. The specter of collapse has even prompted behind-the-scenes efforts by the U.S. Department of Defense (DoD) to coordinate contingency planning with South Korean and Japanese allies. At a summit meeting held on Cheju Island in April 1996, leaders of South Korea and the United States jointly agreed to promote a two-plus-two formula, the Four-Party Peace Talks, even as they privately predicted that the collapse in the North could come as soon as 2 or 3 years.[1] Such endgame speculation on the future of post–Kim Il Sung North Korea has become a favorite diplomatic sport.[2]

At the turn of the new millennium, which many predicted North Korea would not survive to see, not only does the socialist "hermit kingdom" still exist, but with its nuclear and missile brinkmanship diplomacy, it has become a focus of regional and global prime-time coverage. The new consensus in South Korean and American intelligence communities in early 2000 was that North Korea would survive at least until 2015.[3] Paradoxically, Pyongyang seems to have turned its weakness into strength by playing its "collapse card," driving home that it is anything but a Fourth World banana republic that would disappear quietly without a big fight or a huge mess, a mess that no outside neighboring power would be willing or able to clean up. In addition, North Korea has catapulted itself into the position of a primary driver of Northeast Asian geopolitics through its nuclear diplomacy. Thus

2

emerges the greatest irony of the region: today, in the post–Cold War world, North Korea seems both to enjoy a more secure sovereignty and pose greater security risks to its neighbors than has ever been the case in recent history.

The premise of this monograph is that for all its uniqueness as a state and its putative political autonomy, post–Kim Il Sung North Korea has been subject to the same external pressures and dynamics that are inherent in an increasingly interdependent and interactive world. The foreign relations that define the place of North Korea in the international community today are the result of trajectories that Pyongyang has chosen to take — or was forced to take — given its national interests and politics. In addition, the choices of the North Korean state are constrained by the international environment in which they interact, given its location at the center of Northeast Asian (NEA) geopolitics in which the interests of the Big Four inevitably compete, clash, mesh, etc., with each other in various issue areas as these nations pursue their self-determined courses in the region. North Korea, per se, is seldom of great importance to any of the Big Four. Its importance is closely keyed to and shaped by the overall foreign policy goals of each of the Big Four. North Korea is thus seen merely as part of the problem or part of the solution for Northeast Asia.

Rather than examining North Korean foreign relations strictly in the material terms of strategic state interests, balance of power, nuclear arsenals, and conventional force capabilities, it is important to question how instances of conflict and cooperation might be redefined in terms of conflicting and commensurable identities. Traditional realist national security approaches cannot escape the reactive (and self-fulfilling) consequences of a state's security behavior for the behavior of its adversary. The issue of North Korea's nuclear program can never be settled without addressing the country's legitimate security needs and fears in strategically credible ways.[4] This is not to say, however, that force ratios and trade levels do not matter, but rather that the contours of North Korean foreign relations are shaped by far more fundamental considerations.

This monograph consists of four sections. The first depicts in broad strokes *sui generis* regional ("near abroad") characteristics for a contextual analysis of North Korean foreign relations in the post–Cold War era. The second examines the complex interplay of global, regional, and national forces that have influenced and shaped the changing relational patterns between North Korea and the Big Four Plus One. The third assesses Pyongyang's survival strategy in both the security and economic domains. Finally, the fourth briefly addresses the future prospects of North Korea's relations with the Big Four Plus One._

THE "NEAR ABROAD" ENVIRONMENT, OLD AND NEW

In these early years of the new millennium, there is something both very old and very new in the regional security complex surrounding the Korean peninsula. What remains unchanged and unchangeable is the geographical location of North Korea, which is tightly surrounded and squeezed by no less than five countries—the Big Four and the southern rival, South Korea (the "Big Four plus One"). As Jules Cambon wrote in 1935, "The geographical position of a nation is the principal factor conditioning its foreign policy—

the principal reason why it must have a foreign policy at all."[5]

Of course, geography matters in the shaping of any state's foreign policy, but this is especially true for the foreign policies of the two Koreas and their three neighboring powers. A glance at the map and a whiff of the geopolitical smoke from the latest (second) U.S.–DPRK nuclear standoff suggest why Northest Asia (NEA) is one of the most important yet most volatile regions of the world. When it comes to the dream of a Eurasian "Iron Silk Road," North Korea's hub position makes China, Russia, South Korea, and even Japan more receptive to upgrading its dilapidated transportation infrastructure. It is hardly surprising, then, that each of the Big Four has come to regard the Korean peninsula as the strategic pivot point of NEA security and therefore as falling within its own geostrategic ambit.[6] Indeed, North Korea's unique place in the geopolitics of NEA remains at once a blessing, a curse, and a Rorschach test.

The world's heaviest concentration of military and economic capabilities lies in this region: the world's three largest nuclear weapon states (the United States, Russia, and China), one nuclear ambiguous state (North Korea), three threshold nuclear weapon states (Japan, South Korea, and Taiwan), the world's three largest economies on a purchasing power parity basis (the United States, China, and Japan),[7] and East Asia's three largest economies (Japan, China, and South Korea). It was in NEA that the Cold War turned into a hot war, and the region, lacking any nonaligned states, was more involved in Cold War politics than any other region or subregion. Even with the end of the Cold War and superpower rivalry, the region is still distinguished by continuing, if somewhat anachronistic, Cold War

5

alliance systems linking the two Koreas, Japan, China, and the United States in a bilateralized regional security complex.

NEA is more than a geographical entity. Although geographical proximity is important, defining East Asia or especially NEA in these terms alone is problematic because any strictly geographical approach would obscure rather than reveal the critical role of the United States in Northeast Asian international relations.[8] NEA is considered to be vitally important to America's security and economic interests, and the U.S. role remains a crucial factor (perhaps the most crucial) in the regional geostrategic and geo-economic equations. The United States, by dint of its deep interest and involvement in Northeast Asian geopolitics and geo-economics, deploys some 100,000 troops in the Asia-Pacific region, concentrated mostly in Japan and South Korea.[9]

As this might suggest, the divide in NEA between regional and global politics is blurred substantially, if not completely erased, for several reasons. First, the region is the "strategic home" of three of the five permanent members of the United Nations Security Council (UNSC), which are also three of the five original nuclear weapon states shielded by the two-tiered, discriminatory Non-Proliferation Treaty (NPT) regime. Second, Japan, Greater China, and South Korea alone accounted for about 25 percent of the world gross domestic product (GDP) in 2000. As of mid-2005, NEA is home to the world's four largest holders of foreign exchange reserves: Japan ($825.0 billion), China ($711.0 billion), Taiwan ($253.6 billion), and South Korea ($205.7 billion).[10] In addition, Japan remains the world's second largest financial contributor to the United Nations (UN) and its associated specialized agencies. Finally, the rapid rise of China's economic power and related military power has given rise to many debates among specialists and policymakers over how much influence Beijing actually exerts in NEA and what this means for U.S. interests as well as an emerging Northeast Asian order.[11]

The structural impact of power transition and globalization seems to have accentuated the uncertainties and complexities of great power politics in the region. The centripetal forces of increasing economic interaction and interdependence are straining against the centrifugal forces tending toward protection of national identity and sovereignty, not to mention the widely differing notions of conflict management in NEA. In the absence of superpower conflict, the foreign policies of the two Koreas and the Big Four are subject to competing pressures, especially the twin pressures of globalization from above and localization from below. All are experiencing wrenching national identity difficulties in adjusting to post–Cold War realignments, and all are in flux regarding their national identities and how these relate to the region as a whole.

Thus policymakers in Pyongyang—no less than scholars and policymakers elsewhere—are challenged by a unique and complex cocktail of regional characteristics: high capability, abiding animus, deep albeit differentiated entanglement of the Big Four in Korean affairs, North Korea's recent emergence as a nuclear loose cannon, the absence of multilateral security institutions, the rise of America's unilateral triumphalism, growing economic integration and regionalization, and the resulting uncertainties and unpredictability in the international politics of NEA. Regional cooperation to alleviate the security dilemma or to establish a viable security community is not impossible, but it is more difficult to accomplish when the major regional actors are working under the long shadows of historical enmities and contested political identities.

NORTH KOREA AND THE BIG FOUR PLUS ONE

China and North Korea.

Without a doubt, China holds greater importance in North Korea's foreign policy than the DPRK holds in Chinese foreign policy. China's potential trump cards in Korean affairs are legion, including demographic weight as the world's most populous country, territorial size and contiguity, military power as the world's third-largest nuclear weapons state after the United States and Russia, veto power in the UNSC, new market power as the world's fastest growing economy, and the traditional Confucian cultural influence with strong historical roots.

Moreover, in describing relations between the People's Republic of China (PRC or China) and the Democratic People's Republic of Korea, the term "bilateral" is somewhat of a misnomer. Since the end of the Cold War and the demise of global socialist ideology, Sino-North Korean relations have developed with a constant eye toward both South Korea (ROK or Republic of Korea) and the United States. While the relationship between Beijing and Pyongyang remains a special one, its unique characteristics are now defined by China's use of its connections with the DPRK for the maintenance of domestic and "near abroad" stability rather than for any grander ambitions.

Political and Diplomatic Interaction. During the Cold War, North Korea's geostrategic importance and its proximity to China and the Soviet Union made it easier for Pyongyang to cope with the twin abandonment/entrapment security dilemmas. With the rise of the Sino–Soviet dispute in the late 1950s and the eruption of open conflict in the 1960s, Kim Il Sung made a virtue of necessity by manipulating his country's strategic relations with Moscow and Beijing in a self-serving manner. He took sides when necessary on particular issues, always attempting to extract maximum payoffs in economic, technical, and military aid, but never completely casting his lot with one over the other.

In the 1980s, however, the PRC and DPRK were on separate and less entangled trajectories. If the central challenge of post-Mao Chinese foreign policy was how to make the world congenial for its resurgent modernization drive via reform and opening to the capitalist world system, then Pyongyang's top priority, at least in the 1980s, was to contain, isolate, and destabilize South Korea in the seemingly endless pursuit of absolute one-nation legitimation and Korean reunification on its own terms. The 1983 Rangoon bombing (in which 17 members of South Korean President Chun Doo Hwan's delegation were killed) and the 1987 mid-air sabotage of a Korean Air jetliner (which claimed the lives of all 115 people aboard) brought into sharp relief the vicious circle of the politics of competitive legitimation and delegitimation on the Korean peninsula.

During the long Deng decade, Beijing's Korea policy evolved through several phases—from the familiar one-Korea (pro-Pyongyang) policy, to a one-Korea *de jure*/two-Koreas de facto policy, and finally to a policy of two Koreas de facto and *de jure*. The decision to normalize relations with South Korea, finalized in August 1992, was the culmination of a gradual process of balancing and adjusting post-Mao foreign policy to the logic of changing domestic, regional, and global situations.[12] The Sino–ROK normalization was made possible by the mutual acceptance of differences in political identity following China's long-standing Five Principles of Peaceful Coexistence and Seoul's *Nordpolitik*, which called for the improvement of inter-Korean relations as well as South Korea's relations with socialist countries in conformity with the principles of equality, respect, and mutual prosperity, irrespective of political and ideological differences. Ironically, but not surprisingly, the greater challenge has been to China and the DPRK in adjusting their socialist identities in the post–Cold War (and post-Socialist) world.

Perhaps because of the lack of change in Pyongyang's international course, Beijing did not pursue a truly active geostrategic engagement as part of its approach to the Korean peninsula after the normalization of relations with the ROK. Instead, it more or less followed Deng Xiaoping's foreign policy axiom of "hiding its light under a bushel," not placing itself on the front lines of the Korean conflict. While the 1992 two-Koreas decision was arguably the most significant reorientation of post–Cold War Chinese foreign policy in the Northeast Asian region, it did not signal a greater Chinese conflict management role in regional or global politics. China's hands-off approach was demonstrated particularly in the 1993–94 U.S.-DPRK nuclear standoff, when Beijing played neither mediator nor peacemaker for fear it might get burned if something went wrong. The Chinese repeated the familiar refrain that "the issue was a direct matter between the DPRK and the three sides—the International Atomic Energy Agency (IAEA), the United States, and the Republic of Korea."[13] This "who me?" posture reflected a cost-benefit calculus intended to keep the PRC out of harm's way while still holding both Pyongyang and Seoul within its Sinocentric circle of influence in East Asia. Even after Pyongyang's alleged confession of the existence of a highly enriched uranium (HEU) program, China persisted in its risk-averse posture toward the nuclear issue on the Korean peninsula.

Security Interaction. All of this changed, and changed dramatically, in the heat of the second U.S.-DPRK nuclear confrontation in early 2003. China suddenly launched an unprecedented flurry of mediation diplomacy. While the idea of a nuclear-free Korean peninsula is important, for the Chinese leadership and most Chinese strategic analysts, the survival of the North Korean regime and the reform of North Korea are China's greatest challenge and prime objective, respectively.[14] Growing fears of the potential for reckless action by the United States and North Korea as they engage in mutual provocation—which could trigger another war in China's strategic backyard—have served as the most decisive proximate catalyst for Beijing's hands-on conflict management diplomacy.

There were other catalysts for the shift, including China's own enhanced geopolitical and economic leverage, the steady rise of regional and global multilateralism in Chinese foreign policy thinking and behavior, and the creeping unilateralism under the Clinton administration that expanded under the Bush administration. In short, the unique confluence of both proximate and underlying factors—greater danger, greater stakes, and greater leverage—explains why Beijing was spurred into action in early 2003.

With its conflict management resources, both diplomatic and economic, China has clearly made a heavy investment in prompting the Six-Party process toward a negotiated solution or at the very least in averting its collapse. From the beginning, China's mediation-cum-conflict management diplomacy required shuttle/visitation diplomacy — and aid diplomacy — to bring the DPRK to a negotiating table in Beijing. From early 2003 to late 2005, senior Chinese officials have stepped up shuttle/visitation diplomacy on a quarterly basis. Moreover, these visits have been conducted at levels senior enough to require meetings with Chairman Kim Jong Il, serving notice to Washington that direct interaction with the Chairman is the shortest way toward progress in the Six-Party process. The Chinese are reported to have made an exceptional effort in the fourth round of talks — the most important and extended round to date — mobilizing a professional work team of about 200 experts from nine departments or bureaus in the Ministry of Foreign Affairs. These diplomats all spent day and night working on successive drafts of a joint statement of principles, pulling together the lowest common denominator among views laid out by the six parties in the behind-the-scenes negotiations, which included an unprecedented half-dozen bilateral meetings between U.S. and North Korean diplomats.[15]

Caught in diplomatic gridlock and against the backdrop of being labeled an "outpost of tyranny" by the second-term Bush administration, Pyongyang raised the ante of its brinkmanship with a statement on February 10, 2005, that it had "manufactured nukes for self-defense to cope with the Bush administration's evermore undisguised policy to isolate and stifle the DPRK" and that it was therefore "compelled to suspend participation in the [Six Party] talks for an indefinite period."[16]

Pyongyang's decision to rejoin the Six Party talks after a 13-month hiatus can be partially attributed to the synergy of Chinese and South Korean mediation diplomacy aimed at providing a face-saving exit from the trap of mutual U.S.-DPRK creation. This was particularly important in the wake of the Bush administration's characterization of Kim Jong Il as a "tyrant" and U.S. Secretary of Defense Condoleezza Rice's labeling of North Korea as an "outpost of tyranny." Beijing, Seoul, and Moscow have been prodding the Bush administration to stop using this kind of language and to map out detailed economic and security incentives as quid pro quo for North Korea's nuclear disarmament. The implicit withdrawal of vilifying rhetoric was quite important in Pyongyang, as made evident in an official statement of the DPRK Ministry of Foreign Affairs:

> . . . the U.S. side at the contact made between the heads of both delegations in Beijing Saturday clarified that it would recognize the DPRK as a sovereign state, not to invade it, and hold bilateral talks within the framework of the Six Party talks, and the DPRK side interpreted it as a retraction of its remark designating the former as an "outpost of tyranny" and decided to return to the Six Party talks.[17]

The "words for words" and "action for action" approach that North Korea assumed as its negotiating stance and that China inferred as group consensus in the Chairman's statement at the end of the third round of talks, also provided an incentive for Pyongyang, if not for Washington. China was the most critical factor in achieving a group consensus in the form of the Joint Statement of Principles issued by the participants in the fourth round of Six Party talks on September 19, 2005, the first-ever successful outcome of the on-again, off-again multilateral dialogue of more than 2 years. This was a validation of the negotiated approach to the second nuclear standoff on the Korean peninsula that both Pyongyang and Washington have resisted at various times.

China also may have played a critical backstage role in persuading Pyongyang to moderate provocative rhetoric or action. China played a further role in downsizing Pyongyang's demand for a nonaggression treaty, a demand that initially had called for a security pledge or guarantee as well as the removal of the DPRK from the U.S. list of terrorist states. However, Chinese persuasive power has had very real limits. China's efforts to dissuade North Korea from carrying out nuclear or missile tests did not prevent Pyongyang from detonating a nuclear device on October 9, 2006, or launching a *Taipodong II* (along with six other missiles of different types) on July 5, 2006.

In sum, China's mediation diplomacy since early 2003 has been the primary factor in facilitating and energizing multilateral dialogues among the Northeast Asian states concerned in the nuclear standoff. Whereas in 1994 China wanted the United States and the DPRK to handle their dispute bilaterally, from 2003 to 2005 China succeeded in drawing North Korea into a unique regional, multilateral setting that Pyongyang—as well as Beijing—had previously foresworn in a quest for direct bilateral negotiations with the United States.

Economic Interaction. Chinese–North Korean economic relations over the years are notable in several respects. First, Sino-DPRK trade is closely keyed to and determined by turbulent political trajectories. The Chinese percentage of total North Korean foreign trade has fluctuated greatly over the years: (1) 25–60 percent (the absolute value was around U.S.$100 million) in the 1950s; (2) about 30 percent in the 1960s until 1967, after which the ratio declined to around 10 percent in the wake of the Cultural Revolution; (3) increased to about 20 percent since 1973 (to the level of U.S.$300–$600 million); and (4) declined to the 10–20 percent range in the 1980s, although its total value had risen to U.S.$3–

$4 billion. In the first post–Cold War decade, the 1990s, the ratio started at 10.1 percent in 1990 but increased dramatically to around 30 percent in 1991 and stayed in this range until 1998, even as its total value began to decline from $899 million in 1993 to $371 million in 1999. Nonetheless, due to the renormalization process underway since 1999, Sino-DPRK trade registered a 32 percent increase in 2000 ($488 million) and a whopping 80 percent increase in the first half of 2001 ($311 million) after 2 years of consecutive decreases in 1998 and 1999.

Despite the dramatic increases in total value, the China share declined from 29 percent in 1998 to 20 percent in 2000, only to start rising again, more than tripling from $488 million in 2000 to a new all-time high of just more than $1.58 billion in 2005, demonstrating the paradoxical effect of the second U.S.-DPRK nuclear standoff, which has accelerated Pyongyang's economic isolation due to the reinforced sanctions by Washington and Tokyo, while deepening North Korea's dependence on Beijing and Seoul for trade and aid (see Table 1).

Year	Exports to North Korea	Imports from North Korea	Total North Korean-Chinese Trade	Chinese Trade Balance with North Korea	Percent Change in North Korean-Chinese Trade
1979	N/A	N/A	N/A	N/A	N/A
1980	374	303	677	+71	N/A
1981	300	231	531	+69	-22%
1982	281	304	585	-23	+10%
1983	273	254	527	+19	-10%
1984	226	272	498	-46	-6%
1985	231	257	488	-26	-2%
1986	233	277	510	-44	+5%

Table 1. China's Trade with North Korea, 1990-2005 (Unit: U.S.$ million) (continued).

Year	Exports to North Korea	Imports from North Korea	Total North Korean-Chinese Trade	Chinese Trade Balance with North Korea	Percent Change in North Korean-Chinese Trade
1987	277	236	513	+41	+1%
1988	345	234	579	+111	+13%
1989	377	185	562	+192	-3%
1990	358	125	483	+233	-14%
1991	525	86	611	+439	+27%
1992	541	155	696	+386	+14%
1993	602	297	899	+305	+29%
1994	424	199	623	+225	-31%
1995	486	64	550	+422	-12%
1996	497	68	565	+429	+3%
1997	531	121	652	+410	+15%
1998	355	57	412	+298	-37%
1999	329	42	371	+287	-10%
2000	451	37	488	+414	+32%
2001	571	167	738	+404	+51%
2002	467	271	738	+196	+0%
2003	628	396	1,024	+232	+39%
2004	799	585	1,384	+214	+35%
2005	1,081	499	1,580	+582	+14%

Sources: Ministry of Foreign Trade and Economic Relations, People's Republic of China at *www.moftec.gov.cn/moftec/official/html/ statistics_data*; 1996 Diplomatic White Paper Ministry of Foreign Affairs and Trade (MOFAT), Republic of Korea (ROK), p. 348; 1997 Diplomatic White Paper, pp. 396 and 400; 1998 Diplomatic White Paper, pp. 481 and 486; 2000 Diplomatic White Paper, p. 496; 2001 Diplomatic White Paper, p. 483; 2002 Diplomatic White Paper, p. 497; available at *www.mofat.go.kr*.

Table 1. China's Trade with North Korea, 1990-2005 (Unit: U.S.$ million) (concluded).

Second, as Table 1 indicates, North Korea's trade deficits with China have been chronic and substantial.

During the 27 years from 1979 to 2005, the DPRK has enjoyed an annual surplus for only 4 years. Its trade deficit has amounted to a cumulative total of $4.68 billion between 1990 and 2003—imports to the DPRK worth $6.7 billion and exports worth $2.1 billion. The cumulative total of the trade deficits for North Korea amounted to $3.85 billion during the period 1990–2000, with total imports from China at $5.1 billion and total exports to China only $1.3 billion. North Korea's trade deficit is not likely to improve for a long time, because it does not have high value products to export and because its primary exportable commodities are losing competitiveness in the Chinese market. In 2005, North Korea's trade deficit hit an all-time high of $1.1 billion.

While China remained North Korea's largest trade partner in the 1990s in terms of total value, Beijing has allowed Pyongyang to run average annual deficits of $318 million for 1990–1994, $369 million for 1995–1999, and $423 million for 2000–2005. China's role in North Korea's trade would be even larger if barter transactions and aid were factored into these figures. In contrast, South Korea's trade with China in a single year (2004) generated a huge surplus of $20.2 billion.

Although the exact amount and terms of China's aid to North Korea remain unclear, it is generally estimated at one-quarter to one-third of China's overall foreign aid. By mid-1994, China accounted for about three-quarters of North Korea's oil and food imports.[18] Whether intentionally or not, Beijing became more deeply involved, playing an increasingly active and, indeed, crucial year-to-year role in the politics of regime survival by providing more aid in a wider variety of forms: direct government-to-government aid, subsidized cross-border trade, and private barter transactions.

North Korea's dependency on China for aid has grown unabated and has intensified even in the face of its hardline policy towards Pyongyang's rogue state strategy. Recent estimates of China's aid to North Korea are in the range of 1 million tons of wheat and rice and 500,000 tons of heavy fuel oil per annum, accounting for 70 to 90 percent of North Korea's fuel imports and about one-third of its total food imports. With the cessation of America's heavy fuel oil delivery in November 2002, China's oil aid and exports may now be approaching nearly 100 percent of North Korea's energy imports.[19] As a way of enticing Pyongyang to the Six Party talks in late August 2003, President Hu Jintao promised Kim Jong Il greater economic aid than in previous years. The Chinese government has extended indirect aid by allowing private economic transactions between North Korean and Chinese companies in the border area, despite North Korea's mounting debt and the bankruptcy of many Chinese companies resulting from North Korean defaults on debts.

Despite being Pyongyang's external life support system, especially since November 2002 when the United States halted monthly delivery of heavy fuel oil, China does not, to its frustration, receive as much North Korean gratitude as it would like nor does it wield as much leverage as Washington would have us believe, precisely because Pyongyang knows that China's aid is in its own self-interest. As one senior Chinese leader said to a visiting U.S. scholar in the context of expressing China's opposition to any economic sanctions on North Korea, "We can either send food to North Korea or they will send refugees to us—either way, we feed them. It is more convenient to feed them in North Korea than in China."[20] Thus Beijing is cautious to a fault for fear of provoking and/or causing collapse in the North by withholding too much aid, thereby precipitating a host of destabilizing social, economic, and political consequences.

For the DPRK, the most critical challenge is survival in the post–Cold War, post-communist world of globalization, and its economic relations with China are motivated by this survival goal. To this end, Pyongyang seeks increasing amounts of aid as an external life-support system, hoping to avoid triggering a cataclysmic system collapse.

While providing the diplomatic and economic support to the DPRK that was necessary to infuse Kim Jong Il with enough confidence to remain a part of the Six Party process, China also has made it clear to Washington, Seoul, Moscow, and Tokyo that the peaceful coexistence of the two Korean states on the peninsula is now in the common interest of all, in the face of the alternative of having to cope with the turmoil and chaos that would follow a system collapse in Pyongyang.

In the face of a growing multifaceted sanctions strategy by Washington and Tokyo in recent years, especially the September 19, 2005, Joint Statement of Principles, Beijing's multidimensional support for North Korea has been greatly accelerated. Sino-DPRK trade has more than doubled from $738 million in 2002 to $1.6 billion in 2005 with China's share of North Korean foreign trade hitting an all-time high of 40 percent. More significantly, economic ties in various forms of investment are now expanding—from basic industry to mining exploration, drilling in the sea, and various construction projects including a plan to build a new mass-transportation bridge from North Korea's border city of Sinuiju to Dandong, China, over the Yalu River. Beijing has unmistakably shifted its gears from mere life-support aid to developmental aid in late 2005.

Russia and North Korea.

From the late 1950s onward, Kim Il Sung successfully exploited the emerging Sino–Soviet rift, gaining
independence from both of the two large socialist states.
Moscow and Beijing each tried to offset the other's
influence in North Korea with generous economic
and military assistance. For a time, Pyongyang sided
with Mao against the former Union of Soviet Socialist
Republics (USSR), then tilted toward Moscow in the
late 1960s during the years of Mao's Great Proletarian
Cultural Revolution. Thereafter, North Korea adapted
adroitly to its two patrons, whose enmity and status
competition continued through the 1970s and most
of the 1980s. Moscow's aim was to keep Pyongyang
from slipping too close to China; the Soviets did not
want a new war attempting to reunify Korea.[21] Soviet
diplomatic representatives in Pyongyang became
accustomed to finding themselves severely isolated in
an inhospitable environment.

Regarding influence in Korea, it is likely that Soviet
leaders believed they labored under a permanent,
built-in disadvantage when compared with the PRC.
Nonetheless, because the DPRK proved a useful partner
in confronting the United States and insulating against
U.S. troops in South Korea, the USSR continued to
provide Pyongyang with the technology and products
that it requested. But Moscow viewed North Korea as
a functional buffer rather than as a reliable ally.[22]

Political and Diplomatic Interaction. Moscow's
skewed two-Koreas policy started with a bang in 1990
but ended with a whimper. Ironically, if Moscow was
the chief catalyst for transforming the political and
strategic landscape of Northeast Asia, including the
initiation of mutual recognition and the entry of the
two Koreas into the UN, Beijing became the major

beneficiary, occupying the pivotal position from which it could exert greater influence over Seoul and Pyongyang. As if to emulate Beijing's much-touted equidistance policy, since the mid-1990s Moscow has retreated significantly from its skewed posture, moving toward a more balanced policy as a way of reassuring Pyongyang and thus enhancing its leverage and resuming its great-power role in the politics of a divided Korea.

When the Kremlin announced in September 1990 that it would normalize relations with Seoul, the DPRK said in a memorandum that normalization would imply an end to the DPRK–USSR alliance and that North Korea would have "no other choice but to take measures to provide for ourselves some weapons for which we have so far relied on the alliance."[23] The North Koreans even threatened to retaliate against the Soviet Union by supporting Japanese claims to the South Kuril Islands, and they began referring to ROK USSR relations as "diplomacy purchased by dollars."[24] Moscow responded by admonishing the DPRK that no matter how hard the USSR tried to help its neighbor, it would be difficult to solve its problems until the confrontation and arms race underway on the Korean peninsula ceased and until the North shed its semi-isolation from economic contacts with the majority of developed countries.[25]

The political relationship between Moscow and Pyongyang was defined during the Cold War by the 1961 Mutual Defense and Cooperation Treaty. When the Soviet Union dissolved, Russia initially agreed to honor the USSR's extant treaties and commitments, although they would be subject to renegotiation. Russian President Boris Yeltsin sent a personal envoy to Pyongyang to explain Russia's policy and to probe

North Korea's reaction. The North Koreans considered the 1961 treaty "outdated." Not only did Pyongyang embrace termination of the treaty, but North Korea also dismissed Moscow's reassurances that the Russian nuclear umbrella still covered North Korea, implying a revision of Pyongyang's concept of national security.[26]

What is most striking about Moscow's relations with Pyongyang, therefore, is not that there were vicissitudes and fluctuations throughout the 1990s—for indeed there were many—but that the downward spiral of Russia-DPRK relations resulting from a series of domestic and external shocks has been reversed and put back on a renormalization track since the mid-1990s. The period of 1998 to 1999 was a turning point in Moscow's agonizing reappraisal of its perceived rapidly worsening international environment and the reconstruction of its ruling coalition. The statist balance of political elite interests was shattered by the August 1998 financial crisis in Russia and, more importantly, by the North Atlantic Treaty Organization (NATO)/ U.S. war in Kosovo.[27]

The Moscow-Pyongyang renormalization process clearly gained momentum when Vladimir Putin's vigorous pursuit of realpolitik intersected with Kim Jong Il's new diplomatic opening to the outside world. In July 2000, Putin became not only the first Kremlin leader ever to visit the neighboring communist country but also the first among the Big Four to make an official state visit to North Korea. A year later in August 2001, Kim Jong Il returned Putin's visit in a bizarre 6,000-mile train trip across Russia to Moscow that inconvenienced thousands of Russian rail travelers along the way—it took more than a year just to organize it. This was part of Kim Jong Il's coming-out party, evidenced also in 2000 by a visit to China in May, an inter-Korean summit in June, and a visit to Pyongyang by then U.S. Secretary of State Madeleine Albright in October.

President Vladimir Putin's vigorous personal diplomacy in 2000 and 2001 was a dramatic step not only toward bringing Moscow back into the rapidly changing Korean peninsular equation in order to reassert Russia's great power identity, but also toward countering troublesome American policies. The United States loomed large in the second Putin-Kim summit in Moscow. In the DPRK-Russia Moscow Declaration of August 4, 2001,[28] both parties addressed "international" (read "U.S.") and bilateral issues. Four of the eight points seem designed to send a strong message to the United States: "a just new world order" (point one); the 1972 anti-ballistic missile (ABM) Treaty as a cornerstone of global strategic stability (point two); a Korean reunification process by independent means and without foreign interference (point seven); and the pullout of U.S. forces from South Korea as a "pressing issue," regarding which Putin expressed his "understanding" (point eight). The remaining points have to do with the promotion of bilateral political and economic cooperation, especially "the plan for building railways linking the north and the south of the Korean peninsula [as well as mention of] Russia and Europe on the principle of the mutual interests recognized in the worldwide practice" (point six).

This joint declaration was far more muscular and provocative than the June 2000 South–North Joint Declaration, including as it did trenchant attacks against infringement of state sovereignty under the pretext of humanitarianism and against the U.S. Theater Missile Defense (TMD) and National Missile Defense (NMD) programs. The Russian–North Korean summit captured global prime-time and headlines when Putin revealed that the North Korean leader had pledged to eliminate his country's *Taepodong* missile program—a key rationale for NMD—if Western countries (meaning the United States) would provide access to rocket boosters for peaceful space research. Putin also managed to put Kim Jong Il's "satellites for missiles" issue on the agenda of the G-8 summit meeting in Japan.

Since these mutual visits, Kim Jong Il has stayed in close touch with Russian representatives in Pyongyang and has made visits to the Russian Far East to examine the implementation of Russian economic programs.[29] In August 2002, Putin and Kim held a third summit in Vladivostok.[30] There, Putin allegedly assured Kim Jong Il that Moscow would not support any U.S. efforts to impose a so-called "Iraqi scenario" on North Korea and that Russia would not join any anti-DPRK international coalition. Moreover, Russia would try to help the DPRK distance itself from the so-called "axis of evil" and to escape its U.S.-sponsored international isolation.[31] These commitments are known as the "Putin formula." In connection with the events in Iraq, the Russian president stated: "In recent times—and there have been many crises recently—Russia has not once permitted itself the luxury of being drawn directly into any of these crises," and Putin also promised to do everything within his power "to prevent Russia being dragged into the Iraq crisis in any form."[32]

Security Interaction. New North Korean policy toward Russia can best be described as "old wine in new bottles." It is based on shared geopolitical interests, especially with respect to hardline U.S. policy and the U.S. military presence on the peninsula. It is reinforced by personal chemistry and close ties between Chairman Kim and President Putin, and it is cemented by interlocking institutional networks connecting

North Korean and Russian bureaucracies at the central and local levels.[33]

A common belief in Russia is that the DPRK is a militarily weak state that faces overwhelmingly powerful opponents and truly must fear for its own survival. Therefore, its efforts are viewed as defensive in nature. In the wake of the NATO-led war in former Yugoslavia, Russians were predicting that it was only a matter of time before the United States took action against North Korea.[34] Needless to say, George W. Bush's tough policy toward Pyongyang has driven Moscow and Pyongyang toward closer ties. Russian analysts believe that a more robust Russian presence in North Korea could be useful to Pyongyang and to the peace process on the peninsula because reinforced contacts with Russia would help the DPRK feel more self-confident and consequently encourage it to behave in a more pragmatic manner in relations with other states.[35]

In general, Russia seeks a multinational arrangement for Korean peace and security, and it supports the notion that Korean questions should be resolved by the Koreans themselves if possible. Russia opposes neither U.S.–North Korean bilateral talks nor four-way talks among the United States, China, and North and South Korea, although the latter configuration makes Moscow feel sidelined. Russia asserts, however, that the United States alone cannot untie the "Korean knot" but must rely on a multilateral approach to creating lasting peace and security in NEA. Russian policymakers believe that Pyongyang is genuinely interested in reform but is isolated and paranoid; they argue that renewed friendship and trust between Russia and North Korea will help Pyongyang regain self-confidence and engage South Korea bilaterally in a constructive way, just as in its international relations.[36]

Russia was a serious supporter of the Six Party talks on the nuclear standoff. According to Alexander Zhebin, Russia was invited to join the Six Party talks at Pyongyang's insistence:

> Some observers considered it a foreign-policy "failure" that Russia was not invited to the trilateral meeting in Beijing in April 2003, so when the DPRK decided to ask Russia to take part in the Six Party talks on August 27–29, 2003, in Beijing, this was welcomed in Russia as "a positive step" with a certain feeling of relief.[37]

At times, however, the Russians oversold their case, as when a deputy foreign minister declared, "Without taking Russia's interest into account, [resolution of a nuclear crisis] is almost impossible."[38] Russia has tried to build up its relevance by enhancing its leverage in Pyongyang, mostly by proposing to involve North Korea in its plans to develop a Northeast Asian energy network. North Korea, however, usually detects the transparency of such schemes.

The on-again, off-again nuclear talks have allowed Russia to pursue its goal of working with both North and South Korea. In January 2003, South Korean officials asked Moscow to persuade North Korea to rescind its decision to withdraw from the Non-Proliferation Treaty (NPT). Putin sent his deputy foreign minister to Pyongyang to deliver a message to Kim Jong Il on how to resolve the nuclear crisis. The proposed package included nuclear-free status for the Korean peninsula, a security guarantee for the DPRK, and a resumption of humanitarian assistance and economic aid to North Korea.[39] The proposal never got off the ground, and both the United States and the ROK view China as the real key player in terms of influencing the Pyongyang regime. The Three Party and Six Party talks on the nuclear issue all therefore have been held in Beijing. Remembering its exclusion from the 1994 Agreed Framework and from the Korean Energy Development Organization (KEDO), Russia offered to build a nuclear power plant in North Korea as part of an effort to diffuse the crisis, and a Russian power company proposed constructing a power line from Vladivostok to Chongjin.[40]

Once the Six Party talks got underway in August 2003, Moscow proposed a package solution in close alignment with Beijing's approach. Russia's solution was based on the principles of a stage-by-stage process and parallel synchronized implementation of coordinated measures by the concerned parties.[41] Russian officials have spoken out repeatedly for a peaceful, negotiated resolution of the crisis; they have warned of the dangers of a military solution; they have rejected sanctions or other pressure as counterproductive; and they have opposed referring the North Korean nuclear issue to the UNSC. Russian observers have warned that pressure is likely to backfire by cornering Pyongyang and increasing its sense of insecurity. Moreover, Moscow has volunteered to help provide North Korea with international security guarantees as well as energy assistance.[42]

Sensing that its strategic importance to Russia is growing under President Putin, Pyongyang hopes that Russia will be able to assist in solving several of its problems by providing or creating (1) de facto protection against possible military threats from the United States; (2) Russian backing in bargaining with Washington over nuclear and missile matters; (3) U.S. interest in accommodating North Korean demands and requests as a means of countering Russian influence with the DPRK; (4) renewed Russian military aid, including spare parts for existing weapons and hardware as well as new, more technologically advanced armaments; (5) Russian participation in the modernization of industrial

27

facilities built by the Soviet Union during the early Cold War period; (6) reliable long-term deliveries of Russian oil and gas; and (7) facilitating cooperation with the DPRK by countries of the former Soviet Union.

Russia's involvement in the Six Party talks in 2003–06 was cautious but committed. Although China played the frontline role, ensuring that the talks got off the ground and continued, Russia also came to play an important supporting role. Ranking Russian diplomats described China as a "locomotive" driving the Six Party dialogue, whereas Russia's role was to play "whisper diplomacy."[43] Russia and China did work to coordinate strategically during summit meetings in early 2004; both countries stated their desire to keep North Korea nuclear weapons free.[44] In 2003, Russia abstained from an International Atomic Energy Agency (IAEA) vote on whether to send the North Korean nuclear issue to the UNSC, effectively announcing its preferred support for the Six Party format and for continued negotiation. During the third round of talks, Russia joined with China and South Korea in offering to supply energy—in the form of fuel oil—to North Korea in exchange for the DPRK halting any further development of its nuclear programs. Throughout the talks, Russia continued to supply modest food aid to North Korea and to have meetings with North Korean representatives.

Economic Interaction. Ironically, while Russia was angling with South Korea in the mid-1990s for loans and debt relief, Russia's logic for continuing to pursue relations with the DPRK in the same period revolved around hopes of receiving payments on debts owed to Moscow by Pyongyang. Pyongyang had announced its refusal to repay a (estimated at $U.S.3-5 billion) when Yeltsin announced his intention not to renew the 1961 treaty and to halt weapons and technology transfers.

Although Russia traditionally has been North Korea's main supplier of equipment, petroleum products, timber, coal, fish, and marine products, approximately 70 percent of North Korea's estimated $4 billion debt to Russia originates from unpaid-for weapons.[45]

In the wake of President Putin's visit to Pyongyang, North Korea is becoming increasingly active in economic contacts with Russia, which was exactly what Putin had hoped would result from the summit meeting. DPRK authorities have requested Russian assistance in the reconstruction of a number of facilities built by the Soviet Union in the 1950s and 1960s. The problem is that the DPRK does not have money to pay for the services, insisting on barter deals and low-interest credits instead. However, the Russian government, as it faces persistent economic and financial hurdles, cannot agree to such conditions. Barter is unlikely because of the Russian market economy and the fact that government authorities cannot force Russian companies to accept goods they do not need or want—although there were reports of a developing intra-Russian barter economy in the mid-1990s.[46]

The DPRK has presented a list of goods it could export to Russia in exchange for Russian goods and services, but Russian officials say that most of the items on the North Korean list are of no interest to Russian companies. One possible way out of the predicament is to have South Korean banks and firms provide credits to the DPRK to exchange for Russian technical assistance. Perhaps the most revealing part of the DPRK–Russia Moscow Declaration of August 4, 2001, is embodied in point five: "In order to carry out a series of bilateral plans, the Russian side confirmed its intention to use the method of *drawing financial resources from outsiders* on the basis of understanding of the Korean side."[47] In other words, Moscow and Pyongyang are now looking to Seoul, Washington, and Tokyo to foot the bill. Attempts are currently being made to find interested parties in the ROK.

Meanwhile, Pyongyang has asked Russian authorities to set aside logging areas for DPRK workers in the Russian Far East. Russia needs help with its timber industry, particularly given increased demand from China, and North Korean wages are very low. There was even some speculation in the Russian news media following the summit that Putin had allowed Pyongyang to write off $50 million of its debt by providing free labor to timber camps in the Russian Far East.

The presence of approximately 12,000 North Korean workers in the Russian Far East already has created problems not only because they have sought political asylum, but also because they have become involved in illegal activities such as smuggling and drug trafficking.[48] The Russian press also has reported North Korean involvement in counterfeiting and poaching. In addition to the migrant workers from North Korea, the Russian Far East saw the return there in the 1990s of ethnic Koreans who had been forcibly relocated under the Stalin regime. Native Russians met the returning Koreans with hostility.

Nonetheless, Russia is the only country that might be able to absorb a North Korean workforce that is increasingly without jobs in North Korea. At the regional level, cooperation is growing between North Korea and the Russian Far East; since the Soviet period, North Korean workers have been involved in timber projects in the region, and more recently they also have been active in construction and agriculture. North Korean workers help fill a labor shortage in a region experiencing a population outflow, particularly of working-age inhabitants. In April 2001 Moscow and

Pyongyang apparently agreed in principle to settle the pestering debt issue through a labor-for-debt swap deal, whereby North Korea would cover $5.5 billion in Soviet-era debt during the next 30 years by supplying workers who would toil unpaid in Russian labor camps across Siberia. About 90 percent of Pyongyang's debts to Moscow was covered in such a manner in 2000, to the tune of $50.4 million.[49] At this rate, it would take 109 years to pay off Pyongyang's debts to Moscow.

On the whole, DPRK–Russian economic ties do not look very promising, and the development of serious investment and trade relations will likely need to involve South Korea. Russians complain that the DPRK still wants to build economic relations "along the lines of the old Soviet–DPRK model of getting things free-of-charge." On a brighter note, cultural cooperation has resumed in recent years. Russian performing artists are again touring in Pyongyang, and North Korean students can again be found in Russian schools[50] (see Table 2).

Still, Moscow seems excited about the geo-economic opportunities resulting from increasing inter-Korean economic cooperation, particularly the prospect of rail links across the demilitarized zone (DMZ), which Russia hopes would create a new trans-Siberian freight route linking South Korea to Europe via North Korea and the Russian Far East. The difficulty is in leveling the playing field of the highly asymmetrical Moscow–Pyongyang–Seoul economic interdependence by integrating and reconciling Russia's technical know-how and natural resources, North Korea's labor, and South Korea's capital—as well as Russia's debt to Seoul ($1.8 billion) and Pyongyang's debt to Moscow (about $3–$5 billion)—in a mutually beneficial and complementary way.

Year	Exports to North Korea	Imports from North Korea	Total North Korean-Russian Trade	Russian Trade Balance with North Korea	Percent Change in North Korean-Russian Trade
1990	1,315	908	2,223	+407	
1991	194	171	365	+23	-84%
1992	277	65	342	+212	-6%
1993	188	39	227	+149	-34%
1994	100	40	140	+60	-38%
1995	68	16	84	+52	-40%
1996	36	29	65	+7	-23%
1997	67	17	84	+50	+29%
1998	57	8	65	+49	-23%
1999	48	2	50	+46	-23%
2000	43	3	46	+40	-8%
2001	64	5	69	+59	+50%
2002	77	4	81	+73	+17%
2003	116	3	119	+113	+47%
2004	205	5	210	+200	+76%
2005	224	8	232	+216	+9.3%

Sources: *1997 Diplomatic White Paper*, Ministry of Foreign Affairs and Trade (MOFAT), Republic of Korea (ROK), pp. 396, 401; *1998 Diplomatic White Paper*, pp. 481 and 486; *2000 Diplomatic White Paper*, p. 497; *2001 Diplomatic White Paper*, p. 484; *2002 Diplomatic White Paper*, p. 497; available at *www.mofat.go.kr*; KOTRA at *www.kotra.or.kr*; ROK Ministry of Unification.

Table 2. Russia's Trade with North Korea, 1990-2004 (Unit: $U.S.1 million).

In order for this dream of an Iron Silk Road to come true the Russian way, however, Moscow would have to overcome some major obstacles, including the huge cost ($9 billion); Russia's economic weakness; China's relative advantage in connecting its own railway to the inter-Korean Seoul-Sinuiju line (Kyongui Line), which would make it the gateway for cargo travel from Asia to Europe; North Korea's ongoing economic crisis and unpredictable behavior; and the politics of ideological and regional fragmentation in South Korea. Fearing that the new rail projects would diminish the role of Sea of Japan ports that depend on trade with South Korea, some Russian officials from the territory northeast of Vladivostok are opposed to the development of a new Russian-Korean rail corridor.[51]

Regional relations provide only a short-term basis for economic relations, especially through contracts for North Korean guest workers, but the expanded North Korean presence in the Russian Far East has raised new concerns about Pyongyang's involvement in nuclear smuggling, the heroin trade, and counterfeiting activities in Russia. Russian–North Korean regional cooperation will accelerate with the progress of major development projects such as that on the Tumen River, the Kovyktinskoe gas pipeline, and the inter-Korean railway, but such progress will depend on the ability to attract considerable outside investment, especially from Japan but also from South Korea and China.

Russia's ability to influence North Korea is related in no small degree to its struggle to adjust its national identity. In the early 1990s, Russia was concentrating on becoming a respected, democratic member of the Western community. The United States and Europe were seen as the main political and ideological allies of postcommunist Russia, the principal source of economic aid, and the model for Russian development. This vision drove the Russian Federation and the DPRK apart. Yet, with its difficulties in implementing and consolidating Western-style reforms and the threat of NATO expansion, Russia came to suffer pangs of disillusionment with the West and began to emphasize security concerns in its foreign policy, which became increasingly conservative and nationalistic. In this milieu, North Korea found more favor and solidarity with the Kremlin. The Korean peninsula resumed prominence in Russian eyes, and Russia's involvement in North Korea — but perhaps not yet its influence over Pyongyang — began to renew itself.

Japan and North Korea.

Political and Diplomatic Interaction. From the time it regained sovereignty in 1951 until the end of the Cold War, Japan made little effort to normalize ties with North Korea. There was negligible political or economic gain to be had by establishing official diplomatic relations with Pyongyang, and it appeared that the lack of political relations was not impacting the economic ties that did exist. Japan was firmly enmeshed in the U.S. alliance structure in East Asia and did not want to upset the balance by pursuing relations with the communist DPRK. Japan therefore had scant incentive to deviate from the policy of nonrecognition. In addition, in 1955 the General Association of Korean Residents in Japan (*Chongryun* in Korean or *Chosen Soren* in Japanese) established itself as a pro-North Korean organization and thereby became a de facto embassy for Pyongyang, representing North Korean interests in Japan through lobbying and occasional protest activities.

Once Japan had signed the 1965 normalization treaty with South Korea, Pyongyang had less desire to pursue normalization, given its opposition to cross-recognition of the two Korean states and its insistence on regarding diplomatic ties as tantamount to absolute international legitimation. With a debt of hundreds of millions of dollars owed to Japan from trade relations, Pyongyang also was apprehensive over the prospect of finding itself at a bargaining table where it might be called on to pay such a debt (estimated at $530 million, with Pyongyang initially defaulting from 1972 to 1975).

In the late 1980s, the confluence of the Gorbachev revolution in Soviet foreign policy, Seoul's *Nordpolitik*, and Beijing–Moscow renormalization began to undermine the deep structure of Cold-War politics in NEA in general and on the Korean peninsula in particular. In July 1988, newly elected South Korean President Roh Tae Woo promulgated *Nordpolitik*, a major policy initiative aimed at improving inter-Korean relations by expanding South Korean political, economic, and cultural ties with the Soviet Union, China, and other socialist states. It also urged Tokyo and Washington to develop better relations with North Korea. When Gorbachev formulated a new Asia-Pacific strategy, one of the most interesting and groundbreaking ideas was Soviet recognition of Seoul, which was achieved in 1990, paving the road to Sino–ROK normalization 2 years later. The United States had relaxed its rigid North Korea policy in 1988, creating space for its allies to undertake more flexible foreign policies toward the DPRK.

North Korea, in turn, was watching the financial and political support by its socialist allies recede. In the late 1980s and early 1990s, Japan was viewed as being on a trajectory to surpass the United States as the largest economy in the world and so seemed a ripe target for a North Korean state badly in need of support in the form of foreign capital and technology transfer. Japan, for its part, wanted to be sure that it was in place to play a leadership role in the emerging Northeast Asian order.

Tokyo and Pyongyang, in fact, were both shocked by the outcome of the Soviet–South Korean summit meeting held in San Francisco in June 1990, though for different reasons. The DPRK was shocked by the defection of the rapidly disintegrating socialist superpower (the Berlin wall had fallen on November 9, 1988) from its one-Korea policy and sought to compensate for the diplomatic setback with its own surprise normalization. Japan, shocked by the success of Seoul's *Nordpolitik* and its ability to reach out to the USSR and the PRC, felt compelled to act in the name of regional leadership.

Given the ups and downs of inter-Korean diplomacy, the possibility of either a Korea suddenly reunified under terms favorable to increasingly powerful South Korea or a desperate North Korea lashing out with weapons of mass destruction (WMD) seemed very real. Japan therefore found it increasingly difficult to be a bystander in inter-Korean relations that now had the potential to directly impact Japan or to be the driving force of new and uncertain international developments throughout the Asia-Pacific region. Japan had to contemplate the possibility either of another destructive inter-Korean war, which this time would probably involve Japan directly, or of a sudden reunification with uncertain ramifications.[52]

Therefore, on September 28, 1990, the leaders of Japan's ruling Liberal Democratic Party (LDP) delegation joined with the Japan Socialist Party (JSP) delegation and the DPRK's Korean Workers' Party (KWP) to sign a joint declaration agreeing to hold normalization talks. The most important but controversial provision of the eight-point joint declaration stated that Japan should compensate North Korea not only for the damage caused during the colonial rule, but also for the "losses suffered by the Korean people in the 45 years" since World War II. The Japanese Ministry of Foreign Affairs then conducted a rearguard delaying action for years.

After the eight rapid-fire rounds of talks between January 1991 and November 1992, both Pyongyang and Tokyo backed away from holding any additional talks. With the signing of the 1994 Agreed Framework between the United States and North Korea, Pyongyang began probing into whether Japan might welcome additional talks, but it received only a lukewarm response. LDP leader Watanabe Michio failed to restart the talks, and the 1995 and 1996 editions of Japan's *White Paper on Defense* still listed North Korea as the "major destabilizing factor" with regard to East Asian security.

Three new rounds of talks were held from April to October 2000 in Tokyo, Pyongyang, and Beijing, respectively. The ninth round in April involved discussions of Japan's colonial history and North Korea's abduction of Japanese citizens during the 1970s and 1980s. Japan suspected that North Korea had abducted 11 Japanese citizens from coastal towns across the archipelago and in Europe. In August, at the 10th round of talks, North Korea reportedly agreed to stop demanding "reparations" and to discuss "compensation" instead; Japan offered a $200 million loan and $300 million of economic cooperation aid, as opposed to "compensation." Japan also emphasized the importance of solving the abduction issue, as the chief Japanese negotiator pointed out that any normalization treaty to come out of the talks would need the approval of the Diet, which would not be forthcoming without public support that would be contingent in turn on resolution of abduction issue. At the 11th round of talks, Japan offered 500,000 tons of rice[53] and a very large economic package, as quid pro quo for North Korea's moderation of the missile threat and satisfactory resolution of the abduction issue.[54] North Korean negotiators rejected the offer, and the talks collapsed in only 2 days, with no mention of a date for the next round of normalization talks.

These normalization talks again fell apart because of their failure to resolve two major issues: North Korea's demand for compensation and Japan's demand for accountability on the abduction of Japanese citizens. North Korea persisted in its denial of any knowledge about the abduction issue, while refusing to accept the Japanese proposal to offer economic aid rather than reparations. In view of the uncompromising positions taken by both sides on these issues at the normalization talks, it became evident that the settlement of these thorny issues would require a high degree of political compromise between Tokyo and Pyongyang, probably achieved as a package deal rather than through the piecemeal approach.

Despite the Japanese sinking of a North Korean spy ship in December 2001, the year 2002 under Koizumi's leadership witnessed some progress in relations between Japan and North Korea. Japanese and North Korean Red Cross delegations met in Beijing in April and agreed that North Korea would conduct a "serious investigation" into the matter of "missing" Japanese, and in mid-August the first details of abducted Japanese citizens began to emerge from North Korea. In addition, Pyongyang expressed a willingness to accept Japan's economic aid instead of insisting on "reparations." Against this background, Japan announced on August 30, 2002, that Koizumi would visit North Korea on September 17 for a summit meeting with Kim Jong Il. Koizumi's decision apparently reflected his determination to normalize relations with North Korea, and the historic visit aroused high expectations for a normalization breakthrough. The United States, in contrast, on learning about the surprise visit, is said to have put inordinate pressure on Japan not to move too fast on normalization talks.[55]

In Pyongyang, at the first ever Japanese–North Korean summit, both sides gave ground on bilateral issues. Kim Jong Il acknowledged North Korea's responsibility for abducting Japanese nationals and offered an apology. Providing information about new abductees about whom Japan had not asked, North Korea revealed that out of 13 abductees, eight had died and five were still alive. Koizumi demanded that North Korea continue its investigation into the cases, return those who were alive, and take measures to prevent such activities in the future. Kim pledged not to engage in such an act again, saying that Pyongyang already had punished those responsible. The talks ended with a joint declaration in which Japan promised "economic assistance" in the form of grants, long-term soft loans, and humanitarian assistance via international organizations, while North Korea promised compliance with international law, pledging to take appropriate measures so that regrettable incidents that took place under the abnormal bilateral relationship would never happen in the future. Both countries agreed to fulfill "all related international agreements" pertaining to nuclear issues on the Korean peninsula.

To placate enraged public opinion, Japan dispatched an official delegation to collect further information concerning the fate of the Japanese abductees. Pyongyang told the Japanese team that all eight had died from "illness and disasters" and had not been the victims of foul play. However, there were inconsistencies in the North Korean story that further aggravated Japanese families. The Koizumi government arranged for the five surviving abductees to return to Japan for a 2-week visit in October. Before the end of their visit, Japan announced that it had decided to extend the stay of the five abductees indefinitely so as to enable them to decide their future freely.

Following the summit, the 12th round of Japanese–North Korean normalization talks was held in Kuala

Lumpur, Malaysia, on October 29–30, 2002. At these talks, it quickly became evident that there was a wide chasm between Japan and North Korea on several key issues. The North Korean delegation rejected Japan's demand for the settlement of the abduction issue, contending that it had been resolved at the Pyongyang summit when Kim Jong Il offered an apology with a promise to prevent recurrences. Furthermore, North Korea insisted that it was cooperating with Japan in investigating details surrounding the deaths of the 8 deceased abductees. North Korea also accused Japan of breaking its promise to return the five abductees to Pyongyang after a 2-week home visit in Japan and demanded that Japan keep its promise to pave the way for the resolution of the issue; the Japanese delegation denounced Pyongyang's "criminal act of kidnapping." Japan was also insistent that North Korea maintain the tenets of the Pyongyang Declaration, submit to its responsibilities under the NPT, and not target Japan with its *Rodong* missiles. In response to North Korea's desire to discuss economic cooperation as a priority issue, Japan replied that economic aid would come only in the aftermath of the normalization of Tokyo–Pyongyang diplomatic relations. The talks adjourned without agreement on the next round of normalization talks.

Much of the abductions controversy and the 12th round of negotiations came at the same time as the reemergence of the North Korean nuclear issue. Thus, when Japan–DPRK relations became stalemated after the Kuala Lumpur meeting, there was little external intervention to push them forward, and there was therefore no movement in the normalization talks in 2003. In fact, Japan, because of domestic political pressure, became increasingly anxious about and mired in the abduction issue. Despite Japan's concern about North Korea's nuclear program, the issue of the roughly two dozen Japanese citizens abducted by North Korean agents in the 1970s for espionage training had now come to dominate Japanese policy toward North Korea, to the exclusion of all else.[56]

In early 2004 it became clear that Japan was taking preliminary steps toward the imposition of economic sanctions against North Korea. This led Pyongyang to indicate its willingness to be more flexible on the abduction issue. In fact, Pyongyang agreed to allow a Japanese delegate to come to North Korea to pick up eight family members of the abductees who had returned to Japan. Koizumi, desiring to normalize diplomatic relations with North Korea before the end of his tenure as prime minister in 2006, indicated that his visit to Pyongyang should not be ruled out as an option.

On May 22, 2004, Koizumi visited Pyongyang to hold talks with Kim Jong Il, a second Koizumi–Kim summit in the short span of less than 2 years. Kim agreed to allow the families of five former Japanese abductees to go to Japan for a family reunion and promised a new investigation into the fate of other abductees. Koizumi emphasized the importance of a comprehensive solution to pending security issues, including Pyongyang's development of nuclear weapons and missiles. Kim reiterated North Korea's position that Pyongyang had to maintain a nuclear deterrent but also stated that his goal was to achieve a nonnuclear Korean peninsula. In addition, Kim reassured Koizumi that the North would maintain a moratorium on missile firing tests. For these diplomatic victories, Japan paid richly. Koizumi promised Kim 250,000 tons of food and $10 million worth of medical assistance through international organizations. He also pledged that Japan would not invoke economic sanctions as long as North Korea observed the terms of the joint declaration from the first summit. In return, Pyongyang merely allowed five children of the repatriated abductees to go to Japan with the prime minister.

Most Japanese believed that Koizumi had paid too high a price at the second summit, although they gave him high marks for bringing home the family members of the five surviving abductees.[57] In an attempt to pressure North Korea to make concessions, in June 2004 the Japanese Diet took matters into its own hands and enacted a law to ban certain foreign ships from making port calls in Japan. The law was designed to prohibit the entry of North Korean ships suspected of being engaged in illegal trafficking of money, drugs, counterfeit currencies, and equipment and materials used in the production of WMD. At August 2004 working-level talks, the North Korean delegation refused to address the abductees issue in any new way and was not ready to engage Japanese negotiators on the nuclear issue either. Without a breakthrough in resolving either the residual abduction issue or Pyongyang's nuclear weapons program, the Koizumi government decided not to resume normalization talks.

It might appear puzzling that Japan has tried as hard as it has to normalize relations with North Korea. After all, what could it expect to gain from the process? There are several things. In the first place, nonnormalized relations with North Korea stick out as a reminder of Japan's imperial past, and although there has been a recent surge of nationalism in Japan, there is still a desire among the Japanese public to wipe its World War II slate of guilt completely clean. Economically, Japan is worried that it might not be able to compete effectively on a Korean peninsula where other major powers— China and Russia—have established diplomatic ties with both North and South Korea. In addition, there is a concern among some influential leaders of the LDP and among Foreign Ministry officials that the collapse of North Korea would create enormous economic, political, and humanitarian problems for Japan. This last concern enhances the possibility that DPRK–Japan normalization might be an element in a broader agreement that incorporates a solution to the North Korean nuclear standoff.

Security Interaction. During the Cold War, there was very little interaction on security issues between Pyongyang and Tokyo. Japan was ensconced in the protective shield of the U.S.–Japan alliance system, in which the United States did all the heavy lifting while Japan pursued a free ride policy that fits more closely with mercantile realism, separating economics from politics.[58] Because North Korea's development of missile and nuclear programs was not yet known, Japan had little interest in interacting with the DPRK. Pyongyang, at home in its own ideological alliance cocoon with the Soviet Union and China, had no compelling strategic or ideological reason for diplomatic normalization with Japan.

However, as the DPRK's ballistic missile and nuclear programs began surfacing in the early years of the post–Cold War era, Japan may have been the one country that was more alarmed than was South Korea. Although the Kim Young Sam government in Seoul was concerned over the advancing ballistic missile and nuclear capabilities in the North, ordinary South Korean citizens did not appear overly anxious or threatened. The Japanese, however, having suffered the twin blows of Hiroshima and Nagasaki on the eve of their surrender during the last days of World War II, felt a degree of atomic angst they had never experienced during the Cold War.[59]

Japanese fear became palpable during the nuclear crisis of April 1994, when North Korea removed spent fuel rods from its nuclear reactor in Yongbyon and refused to segregate rods that could provide evidence of a plutonium-based nuclear weapon program.[60] Japanese leaders let out a sigh of relief when the crisis was defused by former U.S. President Jimmy Carter's June 1994 visit to Pyongyang, where Carter's meeting with Kim Il Sung paved the way for the signing of the U.S.-DPRK Agreed Framework in October 1994. The Japanese 1995 *Diplomatic Bluebook*, issued after the conclusion of the Agreed Framework, distanced Japan somewhat from the North Korean nuclear issue. Japan saw its main role as one of cooperation: both in the newly established international consortium providing energy to the DPRK and in the diplomatic realm with the United States and the ROK.

However, the 1998 *Taepodong* missile shock galvanized the Japanese government into action on long-term plans. Tokyo decided to develop and deploy its own spy satellite system to improve its ability to monitor—independently of the United States— developments on the Korean peninsula and elsewhere in the Northeast Asian region.[61] In March 1999, Defense Agency Director General Norota Hosei told a Diet defense panel that Japan had the right to make preemptive military strikes if it felt a missile attack on Japan was imminent.[62] Japan therefore decided to acquire midair refueling aircraft to enable its Air Self-Defense Force (ASDF) to conduct long-range strike missions. Tokyo viewed this as important because of Japan's vulnerability linked to its lack of offensive military capacities that could deter or counter North Korean attacks, capabilities that are possessed by the United States and, to a lesser extent, South Korea. Finally, the Japanese government authorized the Japanese Navy and Coast Guard to pursue unidentified ships entering Japanese territorial waters and to use force against them if necessary.

The historic inter-Korean summit meeting of June 2000 drastically changed the political milieu in East Asia, and Japan's relationship with the DPRK improved as normalization talks materialized in April, August, and October. The dramatic summit diplomacy gave some comfort to the Japanese regarding the prospect of a more reasonable and responsible North Korea. Food aid through the World Food Program (WFP) resumed, and the issues of visitations by Japanese nationals living in North Korea and the investigation of "missing" Japanese citizens were broached. Then, in the wake of the October 2002 revelation about North Korea's HEU nuclear weapon program and the outbreak of the new nuclear standoff, Japan readily agreed to increase funding and research support for the missile defense project. Not surprisingly, Japan, as compared with Europe and Canada, had few misgivings regarding the implications of deploying a ballistic missile defense system.[63]

North Korea's official news media accused Japan of blindly following the United States in pursuing a hostile policy toward North Korea. *Rodong Sinmun [Worker's Daily]* declared that the Korean peninsula's nuclear issue "is not an issue for Japan to presumptuously act upon" because it is a "bilateral issue to be resolved between the U.S. and North Korea." The newspaper slammed the door on a Japanese role, asserting that "Japan is not a party concerned with the resolution of the Korean Peninsula's nuclear issue and has no pretext or qualification to intervene."[64] In addition, referencing national identity issues, it criticized Japan for using "various pretexts and excuses to shelve the liquidation of its past and deliberately slackened normalizing relations" with North Korea.

Following a May 2003 Bush-Koizumi summit in Crawford, Texas, Tokyo agreed to become one of 11 nations—the one and only Asian country—participating in the U.S.-led Proliferation Security Initiative (PSI) to interdict WMD shipments to and from countries such as North Korea. That the emphasis is on the DPRK itself and not terrorism in general is indicated by the fact that the 2003 *Diplomatic Bluebook* lists North Korea ahead of the war on terror and WMD as Japan's greatest diplomatic concerns.

In the summer of 2003, the Japanese parliament passed three "war contingency bills" that would give the Japanese government new power to cope with armed attacks on Japan. Such contingency legislation had first been discussed among Japanese conservatives some 40 years earlier but was shelved because of the possibility that it would violate Article 9 of the Japanese constitution. The threat posed by North Korea and international terrorism, however, enabled the Koizumi government to win the support of the main opposition party, the Democratic Party of Japan (DPJ), for the enactment of this special legislation. The legislation enables Japan to deploy the Self-Defense Forces (SDF) swiftly by suspending numerous restrictions hindering its effective mobilization and operation. Indeed, Koizumi has changed Japan's national security policy more than any leader since World War II. In a 5-year period from April 2001 to April 2006, the Koizumi government was responsible for about 60 percent of the national security legislation or revisions enacted since

Japan's Self-Defense Forces were founded in 1954.[65]

With regard to the nuclear issue, Japan has (1) called for complete, verifiable, irreversible dismantlement (CVID) of the North Korean nuclear programs, (2) agreed that discussions on North Korea's security concerns and energy assistance could be advanced within the Six Party talks after the DPRK agreed to CVID, and (3) asserted that there is no change in Japan's basic positions of settling outstanding issues based on the Pyongyang Declaration and the normalization of relations in a peaceful manner.[66] Japan has also continued to pursue defensive military measures, such as an effective missile defense system.

Alongside resolution of the abduction issue, there is no question that reduction of Pyongyang's military threat remains atop the list of Japanese priorities. Japanese security planners, however, are also concerned that a marked deterioration of political stability in North Korea or a military miscalculation by Pyongyang would invite great power intervention, thereby affecting Japanese interests on the peninsula.[67] Japan therefore has an interest in restraining the United States, especially in a world in which the Bush administration has outlined a national security strategy that includes preventive war as a last resort. The Koizumi administration, for example, warmly welcomed the Bush administration's October 2003 offer of a security guarantee for the DPRK.[68]

Economic Interaction. In general, Japan's economic role is potentially critical in the crisis over North Korea's nuclear weapons program. Most important, Japan has promised North Korea, using the 1965 Japan–South Korean normalization agreement as a model, a large-scale economic aid package in recognition of the "tremendous damage and suffering" Japan inflicted during its colonial rule of Korea from 1910 to 1945.

The aid package would go into effect after the two countries agree to normalize relations, with Japan now linking normalization to a resolution of the abduction and nuclear issues.

Japanese officials are reportedly discussing a package on the order of $5–$10 billion, an enormous sum considering the small size of the North Korean economy, the total gross domestic product (GDP) of which is estimated to be $20.8 billion (as of the end of 2004). There is some fear, however, that a payment of this magnitude would serve to prolong Kim Jong Il's regime artificially without inducing any behavioral changes, or possibly that the funds would be redirected to the North Korean military. To capture the money, Pyongyang has moved away from demands that the package be labeled as "reparations" or "compensation" and also has backed off from its periodic insistence that Japan provide compensation for harms allegedly inflicted since 1945.

There has been little indication of how the normalization of relations would impact financial flows to the DPRK, and this may ultimately be of more importance to North Korean economic development than are trade flows. The most likely initial source of such financial flows would come from DPRK-friendly residents of Japan. Although Chongryun is the most active group doing business with North Korea, its resources are extremely limited, and its political clout has shrunk to near zero. In the event of normalization, Korean residents of Japan will play a role as middlemen for large firms, and local governments and business groups in the coastal areas near North Korea are expected to increase their investment in the DPRK. But here, too, resources are very limited and, in fact, declining. Japanese investors have shown only limited interest in multilateral regional development programs, such as the UN Development Program's Tumen River Area Development Program (TRADP).[69] Substantive increases in the form of direct investment would have to come from large Japanese firms and financial institutions, but this is likely to depend on resolution of the DPRK debt issue. Ultimately, North Korea will have to prove itself to be a more attractive location for investment than China (see Table 3).

Year	Exports to North Korea	Imports from North Korea	Total Japan-North Korea Trade	Japanese Trade Balance with North Korea	Percent Change in Japan- North Korea Trade
1990	194	271	465	-77	N/A
1991	246	250	496	-4	+7%
1992	246	231	477	+15	-4%
1993	243	222	465	+21	-3%
1994	188	297	485	-109	+4%
1995	282	306	588	-24	+21%
1996	249	265	514	-16	-13%
1997	197	260	466	-72	-9%
1998	175	219	394	-44	-15%
1999	147	202	349	-55	-11%
2000	207	257	464	-50	+33%
2001	249	226	475	+23	+2%
2002	135	234	369	-99	-22%
2003	92	172	264	-80	-28%
2004	89	164	253	-75	-4%
2005	60	130	190	-70	-25%

Sources: International Monetary Fund (1992, pp. 247, 304; 1993, pp. 247, 305; 1994, pp. 265, 326; 1995, pp. 269-270; 1996, pp. 275, 342; 1997, pp. 342, 347; 1998, pp. 289, 349) and MOFAT (1998, pp. 396, 401; 1999, pp. 481, 481, 486; 2001, p. 497; 2002, p. 484; 2003, p. 497), available at *www.mofat.gokr* and KOTRA at *www.kotra.or.kr*; ROK Ministry of Unification.

Table 3. Japan's Trade with North Korea, 1990–2005 (Unit: U.S.$1 million).

For the near term, Japanese policymakers seem to have quietly concluded that their wisest course is to maintain the status quo as long as possible. For Japan, the issue of Korean reunification poses a dilemma. While a strong, united, and nationalistic Korea could pose a formidable challenge or even threat to Japan, the continuation of a divided Korea with an unpredictable failed state in the North is no less threatening to Japan's security.[70] The challenge, therefore, is to navigate between the Scylla of a unified Korea, with all its uncertainties, potential instability, and new challenges, and the Charybdis of a divided Korea, with the continuing danger of implosion or explosion in the North.

Hatoyama Ichiro, who became the Japanese prime minister in 1955, took the first steps to initiate postwar economic ties between Tokyo and Pyongyang. But only in November 1962 did Japan and North Korea finally begin direct cargo shipments, on a very small scale. Trade agreements were signed 2 years later, in July 1964, but the impact was small. Economic relations between North Korea and Japan were modest throughout the 1960s but made a large jump forward in the early 1970s. The increase in trade in 1972 and 1974 was due in part to the recognition by Tokyo's leftist governor Minobe Ryokichi of Chongryun — the civil society organization of pro-Pyongyang Koreans in Japan — as North Korea's de facto representative in Japan. The group was granted tax-free status.[71] At trade fairs in Pyongyang, the North Korean hosts purchased all Japanese products on display and ordered more, but they were not forthcoming with payments for the goods. When North Korea defaulted in 1972 on payments to the Kyowa Bussan Trading Company — comprised of 20 large Japanese firms — Japan's Ministry of International Trade and Industry (MITI) suspended all export credits in 1974. Despite the lack of payments, limited trade, usually worth no more than $500 million, continued between Japan and North Korea. After North Korea announced its Law on Joint Ventures in 1984, a Mitsui Trading Company subsidiary backed a gold mine venture with North Korean residents of Japan, and an Osaka-based firm established a cement factory in North Korea in 1990.[72]

Remarkably, in 1993 Japan became North Korea's second largest trading partner after China and soon thereafter temporarily became its largest partner. But overall trade volume quickly began to decline, largely due to the severe deterioration of North Korea's economy, sparked by the withdrawal of Soviet and Chinese support in the late 1980s and early 1990s.

Bilateral trade has declined for 4 years in a row since 2002, reaching a 28-year low of $190 million by the end of 2005. More stringent Japanese port controls have led in part to the acceptance of fewer shipments from North Korea, but, more to the point, Japanese firms that had been commissioning manufacture—textiles and electrical machinery—from North Korean plants found the DPRK too risky and Chinese alternatives too attractive.[73] Although trade levels continue to decline, the concurrent shrinking of the North Korea economy may mean that trade with Japan—particularly exports, which generate hard currency—is relatively more important to North Korea today than it was in the 1980s.

Recently a number of local governments have decided to reconsider their policy of making Chongryun facilities either partially or entirely exempt from fixed-asset taxation.[74] Meanwhile, a Japanese government crackdown on drug smuggling has caused much of the

North Korean narcotics traffic to be rerouted through China.[75] In June 2003, Japan ordered its customs and immigration services and its coast guard to expand safety inspections and searches for illicit contraband on North Korean cargo and passenger ships.

At the end of 2003, Prime Minister Koizumi indicated his intention to consider imposing sanctions on North Korea due to Pyongyang's failure to respond to Japanese requests for quick and thorough action on the abduction issue. Although Koizumi maintained that his government was not considering immediate economic sanctions against North Korea, his chief cabinet secretary did not rule out possible sanctions in the future "if North Korea makes things worse." North Korea's reactions to this possibility were negative; a spokesman for the North Korean Foreign Ministry denounced it as a "wanton violation" of the Pyongyang Declaration, warning that Japan would be responsible for "all consequences to be entailed by its foolish moves."[76]

The amended Law on Liability for Oil Pollution Damage, which took effect March 1, 2005, amounts to a de facto economic sanction on the DPRK. The new law bans from Japanese ports all foreign vessels weighing more than 100 tons without proper liability insurance regarding oil spills. Most DPRK freighters are not covered by the required "Protection and Indemnity Insurance," and they in effect will be banned from Japanese ports. It is unclear how effective these independent sanctions against North Korea will be; they could, in fact, result in China gaining much more influence over North Korea. Some commentators have begun complaining that Japan is forsaking what influence it does have in Pyongyang. Amid declining Japan–North Korea trade, the value of trade between China and North Korea tripled in the 4 years from

2001 to 2004, and it now amounts to one-half of North Korea's overall trade, whereas Japan and North Korea are trading only one-fifth as much as at their peak of economic relations in 1980. Japan simply cannot sanction the DPRK effectively without China's support.

Japan's economic relations with North Korea extend beyond trade and investment. North Korea's first public aid-seeking diplomacy came in May 1995 when Pyongyang sent a delegation to Tokyo.[77] The pattern of Japanese aid reflects developments in the political relationship between Tokyo and Pyongyang; shipments began in 1995 and 1996 when relations warmed and then were suspended after the *Taepodong* missile launch over Japan in 1998 and the spy ship incident in 2001. In the face of North Korea's unwillingness to give up its nuclear weapons program, the Koizumi government announced that it had ruled out the possibility of extending any additional food aid to North Korea beyond that agreed on at the Pyongyang summit.

Japan–North Korea bilateral trade and economic relations have declined surprisingly since the end of the Cold War. Although the level of trade between the countries pales in comparison to that between Japan and South Korea, Japan is an extremely important source of goods and capital for the DPRK. Japan also stands poised to be a major underwriter for economic reforms in North Korea. In terms of engaging North Korea since the October 2002 nuclear revelation, Japan's possible economic aid has acted as the biggest bunch of carrots dangled before Pyongyang in an attempt to ensure peace and stability in NEA and also to improve inter-Korean relations.

In recent years, however, Japan has put in place several laws that limit North Korea's ability to engage in either legal or illegal trade with Japan. The problem is not economic; rather, the question of abductions weighs heavily on Japanese engagement. Many Japanese citizens feel an emotional involvement in the fate of the abductees, not only driven by a genuine sense of horror at the actions of the North Korean government but also nurtured for political gain by the LDP.[78] Although the continuing nuclear issue is also relevant for Japan's normalization of economic and political relations with North Korea, it is really the abductions around which the public imagination crystallizes. The abductions are yet another national identity issue providing a wedge in Japan–Korea relations and preventing the expansion of contacts. Pyongyang, however, prefers to accuse Japan of acting as the "shock brigade" for the U.S.-led "psychological warfare and blockade operation" in regard to its implementation of sanctions.[79] Until political issues can be settled, it is unlikely that there will be any major changes in Japan–DPRK economic relations.

The United States and North Korea.

Without a doubt, the United States remains the most dominant external actor on the Korean peninsula. Although U.S. primacy at almost any point on the globe is widely accepted, the description is particularly apt on the Korean peninsula. By dint of what it is and what it does, Washington is seen in both Seoul and Pyongyang, albeit for different reasons, as having become part of both the Korean problem and the Korean solution. Nonetheless, in the conception and conduct of foreign policy, the United States is impacted on and shaped by the changing dynamics of its domestic politics and regional and global interests, even as local and regional factors have gained greater saliency in the foreign relations of both Koreas in the post–Cold War era.

Both despite and in conjunction with the North Korean mantra decrying U.S. imperialism, the United States has become central in Pyongyang's strategic thinking and behavior, alternately seen as a mortal threat or an external life support system, and sometimes as both. With the demise of the Soviet Union, uncertain aid from China, and increasingly close PRC–ROK relations, the United States has become, for want of anything better, the functional equivalent of China and the Soviet Union in Pyongyang's perspective, at least until recently. However, whereas the DPRK's specialty during the Cold War was playing its allies Moscow and Beijing off against each other to reap economic, technical, and military aid, now it must seek to achieve the same aid—and also international legitimacy, investment, and trade—from a single adversary that is increasingly inclined to use force rather than favor.[80]

The Long Road to Normalization. By the end of the Cold War, the United States had a working relationship with China. The second term of Bill Clinton's presidency would bring about rapprochement with Vietnam, 2 decades after the end of the U.S. conflict with that country. Few, however, predicted a quick normalization of relations with North Korea in the post–Cold War years. The intensity of the Stalinist state's political position made such an outcome seem unlikely; after all, Pyongyang rhetorically disparaged "cross-recognition" of the two Koreas as a move toward perpetual division of the peninsula. Furthermore, the predictions of Pyongyang's probable collapse made a pursuit of normalization seem like a waste of time. Nonetheless, by the late 1990s, as Clinton was preparing to leave office, normalization seemed to be on the table, though events during the Bush administration have been far less encouraging.

In the early 21st century, the U.S.-DPRK relationship is one of a kind. With the fall of the Soviet Union, North Korea is the longest-running political, military, and ideological adversary for the United States, and vice versa. Few other bilateral relationships in modern international relations approach this 60-year history of mutual enmity and provocation fueled and sustained by seemingly immutable antagonistic identities.

From the end of Korean War hostilities in 1953 until the late 1980s, there was no formal diplomatic contact of any kind between the United States and the DPRK. With the winding down of the Cold War and the consequent strategic transformation taking place throughout the world, the Reagan administration launched what was termed a "modest initiative" to start a dialogue with North Korea. Recognizing that Pyongyang's increasing isolation was a dangerously destabilizing factor in Northeast Asia, Reagan authorized the State Department in the fall of 1988 to hold substantive discussions with North Korean representatives in neutral settings and allowed nongovernmental visits from North Koreans in academics, culture, sports, and a few other areas. He also ended the almost-total U.S. ban on commercial and financial transactions with North Korea by allowing certain exports on a case-by-case basis.[81] The George H. W. Bush administration, however, did not continue the initiative.

Then on March 11, 1993, the DPRK issued the 90-day legal notice that it was withdrawing from the NPT, which it had signed in December 1985. The withdrawal was a response to the demand by the IAEA — backed by the threat of an application for UN sanctions — for special inspections permitting unlimited access at any time or place (the first such request ever made by the IAEA). The announcement of withdrawal created an instant atmosphere of crisis in Seoul, Tokyo, Washington, Vienna, and New York, while 149 countries "issued statements denouncing Pyongyang's intended withdrawal."[82]

Despite the prior U.S. agreement on the principle of supplying North Korea with two light-water reactors (LWRs), the agreement stalled in the hammering out of details, dragging on for almost a year. In May 1994 Pyongyang began removing nuclear fuel rods from the Yongbyon reactor without the presence of IAEA inspectors. As the matter came before the UNSC, the DPRK declared that "U.N. sanctions will be regarded immediately as a declaration of war,"[83] though Jimmy Carter subsequently received Kim Il Sung's personal pledge to freeze the DPRK's nuclear program. Somewhat embarrassed, the Clinton administration had no choice but to negotiate with Pyongyang, and it began a 4-month process that led to a written agreement, officially known as the U.S.-DPRK Agreed Framework. Although some hardline opponents of this North Korean policy cried "appeasement," the fact is that in the absence of the Agreed Framework, North Korea might today have 50 to 100 nuclear weapons, rather than 1 or 2 or possibly 6 to 8.[84]

The Agreed Framework realized in October 1994 inaugurated a period of limited engagement between the United States and the DPRK. As a putative solution to the North Korean nuclear issue, the document called on the United States and North Korea to implement four conditions. To deal with the energy crisis in North Korea, the United States was to facilitate the construction of two LWRs, with the first one scheduled for completion by 2003, in exchange for a written agreement with the DPRK on the peaceful use of nuclear energy. Also, the DPRK was to freeze and dismantle the graphite-moderated reactors under construction. In addition, the United States would ensure the supply of heavy fuel oil at a rate of 500,000 tons annually. The United States also pledged that it would not use or threaten to use nuclear weapons against North Korea (i.e., negative security), and the DPRK was expected to engage in dialogue with the ROK. In the pursuit of effective international regimes, the DPRK was to come into compliance with the NPT and the requirements of the IAEA. Finally, the two countries were to move toward full normalization of political and economic relations, beginning with reduced barriers to trade and investment within 3 months of the signing of the Agreed Framework.

Pyongyang was very positive in its assessment of the document. North Korea's chief negotiator, Kang Sok Ju, described it as "a very important milestone document of historical significance" that would resolve the nuclear dispute with finality. The official news media in the DPRK called the accord "the biggest diplomatic victory" and went to great lengths to describe it as an end achieved by the DPRK on its own—that is, without pressure or assistance from China: "We held the talks independently with the United States on an independent footing, not relying on someone else's sympathy or advice, and the adoption of the DPRK-U.S. agreed framework is a fruition of our independent foreign policy."[85]

The Agreed Framework, therefore, served as a roadmap for moving U.S.-DPRK relations toward normalization, starting with the establishment of liaison offices in Pyongyang and Washington (similar to the pathway that Sino–American rapprochement took to full normalization), but because of half-hearted implementation of the agreement on the part of the United States, very little progress was made. The lack of seriousness with which the United States would treat the Agreed Framework was made evident when the U.S. General Accounting Office stated that the Agreed Framework should properly be described as "a nonbinding political agreement" or "nonbinding international agreement" rather than an internationally binding legal document.[86] North Korea, of course, had anticipated that the signed agreement would be treated as a legally binding treaty and has since perceived itself as suffering from a double standard of expectations regarding implementation.

The *Taepodong-I* missile test in August 1998 and the suspicions about the restarting of plutonium processing were accompanied by North Korean rumblings about abandoning the Agreed Framework. In response, Clinton instructed his former Secretary of Defense, William Perry, to conduct a thorough review and assessment of U.S. policy toward North Korea. The Perry process marked the beginning of a sustained effort at the highest levels of the Clinton administration to achieve a breakthrough in relations with North Korea. The Perry Report, issued in October 1999, notes the centrality of the Agreed Framework and calls for a two-track approach of step-by-step comprehensive engagement and normalization along with a concurrent posture of deterrence. The report also divulges that during the process of exploring policy options, a policy of regime change and demise, that is, "a policy of undermining the DPRK, seeking to hasten the demise of the regime of Kim Jong Il," had been considered and rejected.[87]

All of this, however, had much to do with the changing correlation of geostrategic forces in the early post–Cold War years. Amid mutual footdragging Pyongyang began to express its concern openly as the 2003 deadline for the delivery of a LWR approached. On February 20, 2001, a DPRK Foreign Ministry spokesman said,

> If [the United States] does not honestly implement the agreed framework, . . . there is no need for us to be bound to it any longer. We cannot but consider the existence of the Korean peninsula Energy Development Organization (KEDO) as meaningless under the present situation when no one can tell when the LWR project will be completed.[88]

On June 18, 2001, the same source warned, "The agreed framework is in the danger of collapse due to the delay in the LWR provision."[89] Soon thereafter, the terrorist attacks of September 11, 2001 (9/11), produced an overall shift in U.S. policy from engaging adversaries to confronting them.

The footdragging over the implementation of the Agreed Framework was due in part to the expectation — in Seoul no less than in Tokyo and Washington — that Pyongyang would collapse before the KEDO construction program was completed. Yet the delay was not all on one side, there also being some North Korean footdragging. Six months were wasted on an "identity argument" as to what the reactor type was to be called, and then a labor dispute shut down the construction until workers from Central Asia were brought in by KEDO to substitute for the DPRK workforce.

With Bush's declaration of an "axis of evil" in January 2002, the administration's refusal to certify in March 2002 that the DPRK was acting in accord with the Agreed Framework (a refusal which threatened U.S. funding of KEDO), and finally Pyongyang's revelations of October 2002 regarding a HEU program,

Pyongyang and Washington found themselves at loggerheads. After a long delay, Assistant Secretary of State James Kelly went to North Korea in early October 2002 for comprehensive policy discussions.

The Proliferation Security Initiative (PSI) was announced in May 2003, organized around the concept of intercepting ships and planes believed to be carrying illicit weapons material. Then, in the summer of 2003, what were purported to be details of DoD's Korea Plan 5030 were leaked to the press.[90] These strategic documents were an anathema to Pyongyang, which was closely attuned to developing U.S. policy. Both DPRK officials and the North Korean media had long and assiduously followed the U.S. security policy debate and relevant published documents. For instance, after the nuclear standoff unfolded in October 2002, North Korean statements regularly cited President Bush's inclusion of the North in the "axis of evil" and the administration's preemption doctrine as virtual declarations of war that justified the DPRK's withdrawal from the NPT.[91]

By the end of the first term of the Bush administration, virtually all former U.S. ambassadors to the ROK and special envoys to the DPRK (Donald Gregg, James Laney, Stephen Bosworth, William Perry, Wendy Sherman, and Charles Kartman) had criticized the administration's approach to North Korea openly. Charles Pritchard, who resigned as the State Department's special envoy for North Korean nuclear issues in August 2003, said, "We've gone, under [Bush's] watch, from the possibility that North Korea has one or two weapons to a possibility—a distinct possibility—that it now has eight or more. And it's happened while we were deposing Saddam Hussein for fear he might get that same capability by the end of the decade."[92]

If normalization is to come about, security guarantees for North Korea seem to be a necessary if not sufficient condition. The centrality of the DPRK's survival-driven security dilemma is evidenced in comments by Pritchard regarding the 2000 U.S. diplomatic trip to North Korea:

> I am struck by what Kim Jong-il, North Korea's leader, said to Madeleine Albright, former US secretary of state, in October 2000. He told her that in the 1970s, Deng Xiaoping, the Chinese leader, was able to conclude that China faced no external security threat and could accordingly refocus its resources on economic development. With the appropriate security assurances, Mr. Kim said, he would be able to convince his military that the US was no longer a threat and then be in a similar position to refocus his country's resources.[93]

In a 1999 interview, William Perry offered a similar assessment: "We do not think of ourselves as a threat to North Korea. But I fully believe that they consider us a threat to them, and therefore, they see [the *Taepodong-I*] missile as a means of deterrence."[94]

Without U.S. engagement, North Korea seems destined to receive neither the international aid that it needs nor the international recognition that it covets. More to the point, without engagement the DPRK is likely to maintain its bunker mentality, as evidenced by pronouncements such as this one from August 2003:

> The Bush administration openly disclosed its attempt to use nuclear weapons after listing the DPRK as part of "an axis of evil" and a target of "preemptive nuclear attack." This prompted us to judge that the Bush administration is going to stifle our system by force and decide to build a strong deterrent force to cope with it. Hence, we determined to possess that force. ... It is a means for self-defense to protect our sovereignty.[95]

Security Interaction. After President Bush's election, a series of radical shifts in America's military doctrine made it increasingly evident that more was going on than mere rhetorical posturing: the *Quadrennial Defense Review* of September 2001 called for a paradigm shift from threat- to capability-based models; and the Bush doctrine of preemption, first proclaimed at West Point in June 2002, was officially enunciated and codified in *The National Security Strategy of the United States of America* in September 2002. The doctrine was implemented in Iraq in March 2003.

As noted, North Korea pays very close attention to these public policy pronouncements, and it is not far-fetched to conclude that the DPRK's willingness in October 2002 to confess having a HEU program was inspired by the bellicosity it found in these official U.S. policies. While U.S. Secretary of Defense Colin Powell was saying in June 2002 that the United States would be ready to meet with the DPRK "any time, any place, without precondition," Robert Gallucci, America's chief negotiator for the Agreed Framework, claims that the North Koreans interpreted this as a willingness on the part of Washington "to meet to accept North Korean surrender."[96] In fact, as the United States was moving toward talks with the DPRK, in August 2002 the administration demanded that improvements be seen in relations between North Korea and Japan. With the second nuclear standoff, the United States has declared the Agreed Framework "effectively dead."[97]

To resolve the nuclear standoff that began in October 2002, the DPRK Ministry of Foreign Affairs issued a comprehensive and authoritative statement on October 25, detailing its version of what had actually occurred in the Kelly–Kang exchanges behind the scenes a few weeks earlier, and also describing the "grand bargain" offered by the North Korean negotiators to U.S. Assistant Secretary of the State James Kelly:

> The DPRK, with greatest magnanimity, clarified that it was ready to seek a negotiated settlement of this issue on the following three conditions: firstly, if the U.S. recognizes the DPRK's sovereignty; secondly, if it assures the DPRK of nonaggression; and thirdly, if the U.S. does not hinder the economic development of the DPRK. . . . If the U.S. legally assures the DPRK of nonaggression, including the nonuse of nuclear weapons against it by concluding . . . a treaty, the DPRK will be ready to clear the former of its security concerns.[98]

There were no explicit calls for financial compensation from the United States. Subsequent North Korean pronouncements essentially adhered to the proposals outlined in the October 25 statement.

At the first round of the Six Party talks in Beijing in August 2003, the DPRK offered a "package solution" deal. The DPRK offered to revive the Agreed Framework—without specifically referring to it as such—and to include a missile deal in exchange for the establishment of diplomatic relations with the United States and Japan, along with guarantees of economic cooperation between the DPRK and Japan and between the DPRK and the ROK. Pyongyang suggested that the dismantling of its nuclear program was contingent on a lessening of U.S. hostility, that a nonaggression treaty was the benchmark of this lessening of hostility, that such a treaty must be of binding legal force, and that action must be taken simultaneously—"word for word, action for action."[99] The North Koreans claimed that China, Russia, and South Korea were open to the package solution, whereas Japan and the United States remained focused on their own individual objectives.

To solve the nuclear standoff by taking account of North Korea's security concerns, the United States did explore the possibility of a multilateral security pact. Powell said in October 2003, "It would be something that would be public, something that would be written, something that I hope would be multilateral."[100] Powell's staff was drafting sample agreements that he hoped would be acceptable to Pyongyang and would ease the impasse over its nuclear weapons programs. In the same month, President Bush indicated for the first time that the United States would offer a multilateral security guarantee to be signed by Pyongyang's Northeast Asian neighbors and by Washington. Pyongyang responded quickly with a cautiously positive reaction. Through its UN mission, North Korea said, "We are ready to consider Bush's remarks on the 'written assurances of nonaggression' if they are based on the intention to coexist with the DPRK and aimed to play a positive role in realizing the proposal for a package solution on the principle of simultaneous actions."[101]

In the third round of Six Party talks, held in June 2004, the United States outlined a denuclearization proposal. This proposal seemed like little more than a reformulation of the CVID mantra. North Korea was required to make the initial concessions without any guarantee of reciprocation from the United States. Whereas the requirements for the DPRK were quite specific, those for the United States were more ambiguous. Pyongyang raised the ante of its own brinkmanship diplomacy with the February 10, 2005, statement that it had "manufactured nukes for self-defense to cope with the Bush administration's evermore undisguised policy to isolate and stifle the DPRK," and that it was therefore "compelled to suspend participation in the [Six Party] talks for an indefinite period."[102] The Western news media jumped on the fact that the announcement also contained North Korea's first public declaration that it had nuclear weapons. The February 10 statement generated a flurry of intensive "bi-multilateral" consultations, and China's preventive diplomacy with both Koreas reached the highest levels.

On July 9, 2005, North Korea finally agreed to return for a fourth round of the Six Party talks later in the month. Suggesting there was no behind-the-scenes Chinese pressure, the DPRK showcased this break-through as stemming from bilateral "negotiations" between U.S. Assistant Secretary of State Christopher Hill (who replaced James Kelly as America's top negotiator at the Six Party talks) and Kim Kye Gwan of the DPRK.[103] Tellingly, Kim Kye Gwan conveyed his government's definitive and date-specific decision to return to the Six Party talks in the course of a 3-hour dinner meeting with Hill, an event hosted by the Chinese in Beijing on the eve of a scheduled trip to Pyongyang by Tang Jiaxuan (state counselor and former foreign minister) as part of Chinese efforts to bridge differences between the United States and the DPRK.

The Bush administration's sudden escalation of verbal attacks on North Korea's long-known counterfeiting, drug trafficking, and other crimes in the wake of the September 19, 2006, *Joint Statement of Principles* may have caught some observers by surprise, but it was hardly surprising for many others. Predictably, the result was to scuttle and replace a new round of the Six Party talks with another round of the Washington-Pyongyang war of words, as Washington and Pyongyang unleashed verbal attacks on each other over activities outside the scope of the Six Party negotiations. North Korea's human rights abuses and criminal activities have been known for years, and yet Washington has dealt with these issues apart from the Six Party talks because it always considered ending North Korea's nuclear program to be its highest policy priority. By the end of 2005, even further delay appeared possible in negotiating implementation of the *Joint Statement of Principles* to eliminate Pyongyang's nuclear program through a "words for words" and "action for action" process stipulated in the document.[104]

More to the point, however, both Pyongyang and Washington showed little trust toward each other. "While in Washington the North Korean nuclear threat has been a major issue for the past decade," as Gavan McCormack reminds us, "in Pyongyang the U.S. nuclear threat has been the issue for the past 50 years. North Korea's uniqueness in the nuclear age lies first of all in the way it has faced and lived under the shadow of nuclear threat for longer than any other nation."[105] With the coming of the Bush administration, Pyongyang has had even more reason to distrust Washington, given the way the United States first appropriated North Korean national identity by making it a charter member of the "axis of evil" and then pursued a hardline policy (although this has proceeded in fits and starts due in no small measure to America's ongoing challenges in Iraq, the first test case of the Bush doctrine for the three charter members of the "axis of evil").

Economic Interaction. Following North Korea's invasion of the South in June 1950, the United States imposed a nearly complete economic embargo on the DPRK. During the next 4 decades, the scope and specificity of U.S. sanctions steadily expanded. Article II of the U.S.-DPRK Agreed Framework of 1994 stated, "Within 3 months of the day of this Document, both sides will reduce barriers to trade and investment, including restrictions on telecommunications services, and financial transactions." In March 1995, the U.S. Department of Commerce approved the sale of 55,000 tons of corn to North Korea by a U.S. grain dealer, opening the door to U.S. exports to the DPRK. In the mid-1990s, Washington approved a number of transactions on a case-by-case basis, including telecommunications link-ups, tourist excursions, airline overflight payments, purchases of North Korean magnesite, and a grain-for-zinc barter deal.[106] Finally, in September 1999, almost 50 years after the initial export embargo, President Bill Clinton announced that the United States would ease economic sanctions against North Korea affecting most trade and travel, thereby ending the longest-standing trade embargo in U.S. history. Many items that had previously required a license were now eligible for export without a license; certain items on the Commerce Control List (CCL) moved from a policy of denial status to case-by-case review.

Today, trade and related transactions generally are allowed for non–dual-use goods (dual-use goods are those that may have both civilian and military uses) if a set of overarching conditions is met. To lift all export controls applied to North Korea, Pyongyang first would have to be removed from the State Department list of countries supporting acts of international terrorism. The United States also cannot extend Normal Trade Relations status—formerly called Most-Favored Nation status—to North Korea because of the restrictions included in the 1951 Trade Agreement Extension Act that prohibited extending such status to communist states. Pursuant to the Trade Act of 1974, this lack of status also excludes the DPRK from the Generalized System of Preferences (GSP). U.S. citizens may, however, travel to North Korea, and there are no restrictions on the amount of money one may spend in transit or while there. Assets frozen prior to June 19, 2000, remain frozen.

Despite the easing of most trade restrictions, trade and investment between North Korea and the United States has remained virtually nonexistent and also highly politicized. As shown in Table 4, U.S.-DPRK trade is almost entirely in one direction: the United States exports moderate amounts of mostly agricultural goods to North Korea and imports virtually nothing from the DPRK. South Korea's trade with the United States in a single day in 2005 ($196 million) is almost two times greater than the combined total of North Korea's trade with the United States in the 16-year period 1990-2005 ($100 million). America's economic sanctions have certainly denied Pyongyang access to the world's largest market, but North Korea has met with only limited success in selling its products in other markets where no sanctions existed.

The history of U.S.-Korean relations — especially U.S.-DPRK relations, from the *General Sherman* incident to the recent standoffs over North Korea's nuclear pursuits — teaches us that the conflict between the United States and North Korea often goes beyond considerations of power. The U.S.-DPRK conflict has deep historical roots born in war and perpetuated for more than half a century. The present conflict is not simply about nuclear weapons but rather about competing worldviews and perceptions of self and others. Rhetorically, it is as much about putative good and evil as about international security. The war on terror that has followed from the 9/11 attacks has involved a Manichean lens in which states are either with the United States or against it. Because of the history of conflict, the DPRK automatically made the "against the United States" list.

Year	Exports to North Korea	Imports from North Korea	Total North Korean- U.S. Trade	U.S. Trade Balance with North Korea	Percent Change in North Korean- U.S. Trade
1990	0.03	0.0	0.03	0.03	N/A
1991	0.1	0.1	0.2	0	+567%
1992	0.1	0.0	0.1	0.1	-50%
1993	2.0	0.0	2.0	2.0	+1900%
1994	0.2	0.0	0.2	0.2	-90%
1995	11.6	0.0	11.6	11.6	+5700%
1996	0.5	0.0	0.5	0.5	-96%
1997	2.5	0.0	2.5	2.5	+400%
1998	4.4	0.0	4.4	4.4	+76%
1999	11.3	0.0	11.3	11.3	+157%
2000	2.7	0.1	2.8	2.6	-75%
2001	0.5	0.0	0.5	0.5	-82%
2002	25.1	0.1	25.2	25.0	+4940%
2003	8.0	0.0	8.0	8.0	-68%
2004	23.8	1.5	25.3	22.3	+216%
2005	5.8	0.0	5.8	5.8	-77%

Sources: International Monetary Fund 1992, p. 247; 1993, p. 247; 1994, p. 265; 1995, p. 269; 1996, p. 275; 1997, p. 347; 1998, p. 280; MOFAT, 1998, pp. 396, 401; 1999, pp. 481, 486; 2001, p. 497; available at *www.mofat.go.kr/*; KOTRA at *www.kotra.or.kr*; United States Department of Commerce; International Trade Administration at *www.ita.doc.gov*.

Table 4. U.S. Trade with North Korea, 1990-2005 (Units: U.S.$1 million).

In effect, there is a resurgence of national identity at the nation-state level, and the divided nation-state of Korea is watching its two halves officially move closer to one another, while the United States remains a target for both appeals and scorn from both of those halves, to greater and lesser degrees. The United States now risks provoking negative responses from both Korean states if it pursues the wrong path, and it risks losing its place on the Korean peninsula if it is not proactive enough.

Not since the North Korean invasion of South Korea in 1950 after U.S. troops had left the peninsula has the question of the U.S. future on the peninsula been subject to so many possibilities and contingencies.

Inter-Korean Relations.

For nearly 2 decades after the "end" of the Korean War, the two Korean states talked about and sometimes acted out their competing unification visions only in the context of the overthrow or replacement of one national identity by the other. After the shock of President Nixon's visit to China in the early 1970s, inter-Korean relations developed in fits and starts, mutating through four cycles of dialogue and reconciliation.[107] The first cycle, beginning in August 1971, entailed a series of seven Red Cross talks held alternately in Pyongyang and Seoul over 2 years, culminating in a joint communiqué in which both Koreas agreed to uphold three principles: (1) unification achieved through independent efforts; (2) unification achieved through peaceful means; and (3) national unity sought by transcending differences in ideas, ideologies, and systems.

The second cycle of talks, running from September 1984 through February 1986, involved a flurry of contacts and exchanges in various functional and humanitarian fields; these talks reaffirmed the three principles of unification. The third cycle, which began in 1990 and was inspired in part by changes in global politics linked with the end of the Cold War, was more promising than the first two. It jump-started inter-Korean trade, eased the entry of the two Koreas into the UN as two separate but equal member states, and led to the drafting of two documents: the North–South

Basic Agreement (officially known as "Agreement on Reconciliation, Nonaggression, and Exchanges and Cooperation between the South and the North") and the "Joint Declaration of the Denuclearization of the Korean Peninsula."

With Kim Dae Jung's inauguration as ROK president in February 1998, South Korea initiated the Sunshine Policy of opening to North Korea with a pledge not to undermine or absorb the DPRK. The new policy was based in part on explicit recognition that undermining the DPRK is simply not a viable policy option because of the disorder and destruction that would follow from a Northern collapse.[108] President Kim Dae Jung's repeated pledges that the South has no intent "to undermine or absorb North Korea," thus speaking to one of the key remaining fears in Pyongyang, stand out as one of the most significant steps toward accepting identity difference as an integral part of the gradual peace process.[109]

The Sunshine Policy created the appropriate conditions — both in South Korea and in North Korea — for the historic inter-Korean summit of June 13–15, 2000, which catalyzed the fourth and most promising cycle — indeed, a turning point — of inter-Korean dialogue and cooperation. Without a doubt, the chief catalyst for the Pyongyang summit was President Kim Dae Jung's consistent and single-minded pursuit of his pro-engagement Sunshine Policy. More than anything else, the offer of substantial if unspecified governmental aid to refurbish North Korea's decrepit infrastructure was an important causal force behind Kim Jong Il's decision to agree to the summit. Until Kim Dae Jung's Berlin Declaration in March 2000 offering aid to the DPRK,[110] Pyongyang had taken a two-handed approach, attacking the Sunshine Policy as a "sunburn policy" on ideological grounds while simultaneously pursuing a mendicant strategy to extract maximum economic concessions. Before the official unveiling of the statement in Berlin, Seoul delivered an advance text to Pyongyang, Beijing, Moscow, Tokyo, and Washington, demonstrating that the Big Four had little to do with the initiation of the summit.

The 2000 Pyongyang summit was most remarkable historically because it was initiated and executed by Koreans themselves with no external shock or great-power sponsorship. The previous inter-Korean accords had been responses to major changes external to the Korean peninsula, such as the 1972 joint communiqué after Nixon's visit to China or the 1992 agreements following the demise of the Cold War. The Pyongyang summit, the first of its kind in the half-century history of politics of competitive legitimation and delegitimation on the divided peninsula, generated opportunities and challenges for the Big Four as they stepped back to reassess the likely future of inter-Korean affairs and the implications for their own national interests. The dramatic summit also led to some paradoxical expectations and consequences.

Suddenly, at least from June to November of 2000, the capital city of Pyongyang, the city of darkness, became a city of diplomatic light and a primary arena for diplomatic influence and competition among the Big Four as inter-Korean relations returned to a more international field. The notion that the Pyongyang summit had improved prospects for melting the remnant Cold War glacier on the Korean peninsula seemed to have intensified the needs and efforts of the Big Four to readjust their respective Korea policies in response to rapidly changing realities on the ground.

The North Koreans viewed and framed the summit, although native in origin, as a major concession to the United States and as a concrete step taken by the DPRK to fulfill one of the obligations in the 1994 Agreed Framework.[111] The United States was then expected to make major economic and strategic concessions. Pyongyang did its best to exploit the new connection with Seoul in order to speed up normalization talks with the United States and to gain access to bilateral and multilateral aid and foreign direct investment.

In addition to the summit with Kim Dae Jung, the infamously reclusive Kim Jong Il also met first with Chinese President Jiang Zemin in a secret visit to Beijing in May 2000 and then with Russian President Vladimir Putin that July, after which he received a flurry of diplomatic missions to Pyongyang, including U.S. Secretary of State Madeleine Albright, Chinese Defense Minister Chi Haotian, and a European Union (EU) delegation. By early 2001, however, Pyongyang's high hopes and expectations from the "Clinton in Pyongyang Shock" turned into the "Bush in Washington Shock," with low and ever-diminishing returns.

Furthermore, while the Joint Declaration speaks of economic cooperation and indeed has fostered significant growth in that area, it failed to address military and security matters, lacking even a general statement about working together for tension reduction and confidence-building. Pyongyang clearly desired to discuss security issues only with the United States. Tellingly, Pyongyang has held the administration in Washington hostage to the resumption of inter-Korean dialogue, at least from January 2001 to August 2002, breaching not only the letter and the spirit of the North-South Joint Declaration but also its own longstanding party line that Korean affairs should be handled without foreign intervention or interference.

But the significance of the summit should not be underrated. It was all about mutual recognition and legitimation, and it succeeded in no small measure in finally bringing the two Koreas down from their hegemonic-unification dreamlands to acceptance of peaceful coexistence as two separate states. The single greatest accomplishment of the summit was to deliver a major blow to the fratricidal politics of competitive legitimation and delegitimation. Although the two Kims symbolically signaled their acceptance of each other's legitimacy through their actions at the summit, neither of them enunciated a belief that reunification would be coming in the near future. Kim Dae Jung, in fact, predicted that it would take 20 to 30 years for the divided Korean peninsula to achieve national unification, even as North Korea declared for the first time to the domestic audience that "the issue of unifying the differing systems in the North and the South as one *may be left to posterity to settle slowly in the future."*[112]

The Joint Declaration produced by the summit, while initially limited in domain, adopted a functional "peace by pieces" approach to the Korean conflict.[113] In effect, economic relations were anointed as the practical pathway for the gradual development and institutionalization of a working peace mechanism for the two Koreas. The fourth article of the document used the term "national economy," apparently assuming an eventual integration of North and South Korean economies.[114] It is worth noting in this connection that for the period from July 1972 to August 2005, covering all four cycles of dialogue and cooperation, 47 inter-Korean agreements were signed, breaking down as follows: one during the first cycle; none during the second cycle; 13 during the third cycle (December 1991–July 1994); and 33 during the fourth cycle (April 2000–August 2005). Inter-Korean dialogue and cooperation came to a halt during the first 20 months of the Bush administration (from January 2001 to August 2002) — not a single inter-Korean accord was signed — but Pyongyang returned to inter-Korean dialogue in late August 2002, signing no less than six accords through the end of 2003.[115]

Almost in tandem with the simmering U.S.-DPRK nuclear standoff and the coming of the Roh Moo-hyun government, both the speed and scope of inter-Korean talks and cooperation have accelerated, and nearly 100 rounds of official government-level meetings have been held since the inauguration of the "Policy of Peace and Prosperity" by the Roh administration in February 2003. Of course, the second U.S.-DPRK nuclear standoff could overshadow but not reverse some remarkable achievements in inter-Korean relations in all issue areas from August 2002 to mid-2006. With the election in December 2002 of Roh Moo-hyun, an offspring candidate of the "386 generation," North Korea finds "its most cooperative South Korean government ever. . . . Roh emphasized even more strongly than his predecessor that inter-Korean economic cooperation would continue and that dialogue and economic inducements were the best means to bring about positive change in North Korea's behavior."[116] Pyongyang's view of the state of inter-Korean relations also has evolved to such an extent that it could confidently declare in its Joint New Year (2003) Editorial: "It can be said that there exists on the Korean Peninsula at present only confrontation between the Koreans in the North and the South and the United States."[117]

As shown in Table 5, inter-Korean trade registered a 5.2 percent decline from 2000 to 2001 but recorded a huge 59.3 percent increase from 2001 to 2002 and another impressive 51.5 percent increase from 2004 to 2005. In 2005 inter-Korean trade topped $1 billion for the first time, sufficing to make Seoul Pyongyang's second largest trade partner after China. In fact, since 2002, South Korea has become and has remained the North's second largest trading partner, surging ahead of Japan. Inter-Korean trade now constitutes 26 percent of North Korea's total foreign trade (but alas, only 0.19 percent of South Korea's total foreign trade).

Year	Imports from North Korea	% Change	Exports to North Korea	% Change	Total trade	% change
1989	18,655		69		18,724	
1990	12,278	-34.2	1,188	1,621.7	13,466	-28.1
1991	105,719	761.0	5,547	366.9	111,266	726.3
1992	162,863	54.1	10,563	90.4	173,426	55.9
1993	178,167	9.4	8,425	-20.2	186,592	7.6
1994	176,298	-1.0	18,249	116.6	194,547	4.3
1995	222,855	26.4	64,436	253.1	287,291	47.7
1996	182,400	-18.2	69,639	8.1	252,039	-12.3
1997	193,069	5.8	115,270	65.5	308,339	22.3
1998	92,264	-52.2	129,679	12.5	221,943	-28.0
1999	121,604	31.8	211,832	63.4	333,437	50.2
2000	152,373	25.3	272,775	28.8	425,148	27.5
2001	176,170	15.6	226,787	-16.9	402,957	-5.2
2002	271,575	54.2	370,155	63.2	641,730	59.3
2003	289,252	6.5	434,965	17.5	724,217	12.9
2004	258,039	-10.8	439,001	0.9	697,040	-3.8
2005	340,281	31.0	715,472	63.0	1,055,753	51.5

Note: These figures include both transactional and nontransactional (i.e., noncommercial) trade.
Sources: KOTRA at *www.kotra.go.kr*; ROK Ministry of Unification.

Table 5. South Korean–North Korean Trade, 1989–2005 (Unit: U.S.$1,000).

Trade with South Korea is in general de facto economic aid for North Korea, and the ROK has become one of the major sources of hard currency in the DPRK.[118] Beginning in the early 1990s with small exchanges of goods, trade, which was essentially the functional cornerstone of Kim Dae Jung's Sunshine Policy, has continued despite nuclear tensions. Over the course of Kim Dae Jung's and Roh Moo-hyun's presidencies, inter-Korean trade registered a nearly five-fold increase from $221 million in 1998 to $1,055 million in 2005.

One of the key components of this trade is processing-on-commission (POC) trade, in which South Korean companies export raw materials to the DPRK and then import finished or semifinished products. This type of trade involves the creation of new jobs in North Korea, some degree of technology transfer, a fair amount of investment in the North from the South, and, most importantly, direct contact between North and South Koreans. Many of the POC plants that have been established use South Korean machinery and supervisors. By 2003, South Korean companies were making shoes, beds, television sets, and men's suits in the North.[119]

In addition, since the mid-1990s, Seoul has increased its flows of "nontransactional" trade, which is the exchange of noncommercial goods, such as those used in the now defunct KEDO reactor projects or for humanitarian aid. Nontransactional trade began in 1995 and has increased to such a degree that it is about 40 percent of total inter-Korean trade on the average. Overall, these increased trading relations are part of a program led by the ROK but accepted by the DPRK to create functional linkages between North and South in the interest of managing conflict, maintaining peace, and catalyzing eventual reunification.[120]

Although trade may be growing and increasingly impressive, it is investment that will make the most difference for the North Korean economy and for economic relations in the interests of fostering peace on the peninsula.[121] Despite the self-reliant *juche* philosophy that undergirds the DPRK's national identity, the newly-minted Kaesong Industrial Complex (KIC) in North Korea already has attracted attention from a number of small- and medium-size companies in South Korea. The reconnection of roads and railways between the two countries—what President Kim Dae Jung characterized as de facto unification—will reduce the transaction costs of trade and embed both countries in a larger Northeast Asian trading system. Pyongyang has recognized the essential need to open itself to foreign economic agents and has undertaken legal reform to encourage investment and trade. South Korea is the most likely source of the funding that can revitalize or at least stabilize the DPRK's economy. What many realists dismissed as beyond the realm of possibility only a few years ago is now happening, as raw materials and finished products are passing along and through what was once considered a major invasion route.[122] This "peace by pieces" functional cooperation provides ways of living with identity differences on the divided Korean peninsula rather than fighting about them.

In addition, cultural and social exchanges, though not as revolutionary as some had hoped, have continued unabated. Since its opening in November 1998, the Mt. Kumgang project has increased the number of South Koreans who travel to the North. With the reestablishment of road and rail links between the two Koreas, along with the demining of areas of the DMZ around these links, South Korean tour buses made the first overland tours to Mt. Kumgang in North Korea in over 50 years, and the South Korean conglomerate Hyundai continued work on industrial plants in Kaesong in the North. Civilian exchanges and cooperation are surging substantially as well. In 2005 alone, the number of people who traveled between the two Koreas reached 88,341, surpassing the total number of people exchanges for the past 60 years.

The normative and functional spillovers from growing inter-Korean dialogue and reconciliation can be seen in several noneconomic domains. After more than half a century of politics of competitive legitimation and delegitimation, the leaders of the pro-Seoul Korean Residents Union in Japan (*Mindan*) and the pro-Pyongyang General Association of Korean Residents in Japan (*Chongryun*) met for the first time on May 17, 2006. They issued a joint statement pledging to turn their longstanding antagonism into reconcilation and cooperation. The joint statement was influenced greatly by the declared intentions of their respective "home states," being based largely on the North-South Joint Declaration of June 15, 2000. Even in the military/ security domain, rare talks between North and South Korean generals in 2004 (the first of their kind) made progress on the establishment of naval radio contact to prevent firefights like those of 1999 and 2002 and also on the discontinuation of propaganda activities against each other along the 155-mile-long DMZ. As noted earlier, the convergence of the positions of Chinese and the two Koreas in the fourth round of Six Party talks is a remarkable event defying the conventional realist wisdom. Thus in a series of accords and agreements reached over the years, especially from 2000 to 2006, the relationship between North and South Korea has come quite close to that of mutually recognized sovereign states.

EXPLAINING NORTH KOREA'S SECURITY-CUM-SURVIVAL STRATEGY

As is amply made manifest in U.S.-DPRK nuclear confrontations and negotiations—and Pyongyang's "package solution" proposal—there remains the inseparable linkage of security, development, and legitimacy in the conduct of North Korean foreign policy. Indeed, three types of crisis—security crisis, economic crisis, and legitimation crisis—all frame and drive North Korea's security-cum-survival strategy in the post–Kim Il Sung era.

The Quest for Security.

During the Cold War, Pyongyang's main security concern was not so much to balance against or bandwagon with the United States as in coping with the twin security dilemmas of allied abandonment and allied entrapment. Ironically, it was the Sino-Soviet conflict, not the U.S.-Soviet tensions, that most enhanced "the power of the weak." In its security behavior, Pyongyang demonstrated a remarkable unilateral zigzag balancing strategy in its relations with Moscow and Beijing, taking sides if necessary on particular issues, while attempting at the same time to extract maximum payoffs in economic, technical, and military aid, but never completely casting its lot with one or the other.

How can we then explain the paradox of the survival of post–Kim Il Sung North Korea in the post–Cold War era? The literature on asymmetric conflicts shows that weaker powers have engaged in wars against stronger adversaries more often than not, and big powers frequently lose wars in asymmetric conflicts (e.g., the Vietnam War).[123] According to a recent study, weak states were victorious in nearly 30 percent of all asymmetric wars in the approximately 200-year period covered in the *Correlates of War* data set. More tellingly, weak states have won with increasing frequency as the modern era approached.[124] Weaker states also have initiated many brinkmanship crises that fell short of war, a strategy that North Korea has employed repeatedly.[125]

A consideration of multiple and mutually interactive influences can help us answer the puzzle of Pyongyang's uncanny resilience and "the power of the weak" in the context of the DPRK-U.S. nuclear confrontation. Drawing theoretical insight from asymmetric conflict and negotiation theory, we may postulate that the power balance in an issue-specific relationship and the performance of the weaker state are affected by four key variables: the weak state's proximity to the strategic field of play; the availability to the stronger state of feasible alternatives; the stakes involved for both states in conflict and the degree of their resolve; and the degree of control for all involved parties.[126]

As a weaker state in conflict with a superpower and its allies (South Korea and Japan), North Korea has relied upon issue-specific and situation-specific power, the effectiveness and credibility of which has required resources other than the traditional elements of national power. North Korea's proximity to the strategic field of play, its compensating brinkmanship strategy, the high stakes involved, and its governmental resolve and control have all reinforced one another to make a strong actor's aggregate conventional power largely less relevant. North Korea has adopted a wide range of tactics in and out of the asymmetric conflict and negotiation processes in order to reduce the opponent's alternatives and weaken the opponent's resolve and control.

The geographical position of the DPRK is one of the most compelling and immutable factors in Pyongyang's survival strategy. Since countries can change their leaders, systems, policies, and strategies but cannot change their location, "geography or geopolitics has long been the point of departure for studies of foreign policy or world politics."[127] Surrounded by all four major powers and its southern rival, North Korea's home turf is the strategic field of play from which it exercises its brinkmanship or plays its collapse card. Contrary to the conventional realist wisdom, in asymmetrical conflict and negotiations the strong state does not *ipso facto* exert greater control than the weak state. If a smaller and weaker state occupies territory of strategic importance to a larger and stronger state, or if the field of play is on the weak actor's home turf (as was the case in the U.S.-Panama negotiations and British-Iceland Cod Wars), the weaker state can deploy bargaining clout disproportionate to its intrinsic coercive potential.[128]

The ineluctable fact that North Korea is at the center of the strategic crossroads of Northeast Asia where the Big Four uneasily meet and interact has served rather well in bolstering Pyongyang's control. By dint of its proximity to what Peter Hayes called "the fuse on the nuclear powder keg in the Pacific,"[129] Pyongyang has leveled the field of play so as to wield greater control than the United States by constantly changing the rules of entry and the rules of play in the pursuit of its preferred outcome. North Korea's manifest preference for direct bilateral negotiations with the United States also is a way of seeking the home court advantage to maximize its control in the asymmetric conflict and negotiation process.

Consider as well how Pyongyang's geographical position, combined with its military of 1.2 million members and its asymmetric military capabilities, provides ample fodder for its survival-driven leverage diplomacy with South Korea and the United States. Some 70 percent of its active force—700,000 troops, 8,000 artillery systems, and 2,000 tanks—are forward-deployed near the DMZ. Seoul, where one-fourth of South Korea's 49 million people live and where nearly 75 percent of the country's wealth is concentrated, is only 40 kilometers (25 miles) from the DMZ and thus within easy reach of North Korean jet fighters, armored vehicles, Scud missiles, and artillery guns. Within minutes, Pyongyang could turn Seoul into "a sea of fire," as it threatened to do in the heat of the first nuclear crisis of mid-1994. Any ultimate Allied triumph would be a Pyrrhic victory since such devastation would be crippling to South Korea.[130]

Without launching such an armed invasion, Pyongyang could still exercise its "negative power" or even play its collapse card to spawn instability on the divided Korean peninsula. One of the underlying rationales for the inauguration of the Kim Dae Jung administration's "sunshine policy" was that potential implosion or explosion in the North would put at risk South Korea's recovery from the 1997–98 financial crisis by discouraging foreign direct investment inflows. The financial crisis served as a wake-up call regarding the consequences of North Korea's prospective collapse. Hence, to deter or delay the economic effects of a North Korean hard landing as long as possible, the sunshine policy became South Korea's default policy.[131] In March 2005 President Roh Moo-hyun publicly declared, "We will not be embroiled in any [armed] conflict in Northeast Asia against our will. This is an absolutely firm principle we cannot yield under any circumstances."[132]

North Korea's geographical location is also of considerable strategic concern to NEA's Big Four. Located at the pivot point of the NEA security complex and at the most important strategic nexus of the Asia-Pacific region, Pyongyang is capable, by hostility or instability, of entrapping any or all of the Big Four in a stairstep of conflict escalation these governments would rather avoid. If Pyongyang's brinkmanship or Washington's sanctions or regime-change strategy escalate to war, the cost to all parties would be exorbitant.

Concomitant to Pyongyang's survival strategy are the limitations of Washington's issue-specific power to pressure Pyongyang and the lack of palatable alternatives to negotiation. The twisted logic of a self-styled *juche* kingdom is that it is not as vulnerable as a normal state to public shaming and the various sanction tools of traditional statecraft. The acceptable nonnegotiation alternatives available to the United States in the resolution of the North Korean nuclear and missile issues have remained severely limited.

The credible threats of surgical military strikes and enforceable economic sanctions against Pyongyang were considered but rejected because of the Pentagon's objections, Seoul's vulnerability, China's veto threat, and even Tokyo's reluctance. William Perry — reflecting on his involvement in the emergency national security meeting of June 16, 1994, regarding the most serious North Korean nuclear brinkmanship crisis of his tenure as Secretary of Defense — writes about a third-way option for a negotiated deal in the face of the extremely limited alternatives available to U.S. policymakers:

"We were about to give the president a [third-way] choice between a disastrous option—allowing North Korea to get a nuclear arsenal, which we might have to face someday—and an unpalatable option, blocking this development, but thereby risking a destructive nonnuclear war."[133] Given all the constraints on America's issue-specific power, the rise of a cost-aware foreign policy, and the collapse of a bipartisan foreign policy consensus in the 1990s, the U.S.-DPRK Agreement of October 21, 1994, could be said to be the worst deal, except that there was no better alternative.

For Beijing—and to a lesser extent for Seoul, Moscow, and Tokyo—Washington's sanctions diplomacy in mid-1994 emerged as a no-win proposition, as it would bring about the worst of two possible outcomes. It could be ineffective in controlling nuclear proliferation since it could only strengthen the determination of the North Korean leadership to go nuclear, or it could destabilize a North Korean regime that would then dump many of its ill-fed, fleeing refugees on China's northeastern and Russia's far eastern provinces. Thus, paradoxically, Pyongyang's growing difficulties and threat of collapse have increased its bargaining leverage relative to its weak intrinsic power.

Another consideration regarding leverage in asymmetrical negotiations is the matter of relative and absolute stakes and resolve. The higher the stakes for a state actor in the process of bargaining, the more it is willing to commit its resources and the greater its resolve to attain a favorable negotiation outcome. The issue of stakes may have a crucial part in explaining why the weaker North Vietnam ultimately achieved victory during the Vietnam War fought on Vietnamese turf. Similarly, North Korea has been disadvantaged against the United States in the overall correlation of forces, but there also remained a clear asymmetry in survival stakes and resolve favoring Pyongyang—to wit, Washington's apprehensions regarding the integrity of the NPT regime. Compare America's relatively nonchalant reaction to the nuclear breakout states India and Pakistan with U.S. nervousness in the face of a Pyongyang bolstered by fear for its survival and consequent highest possible resolve.

Of course, resolve without capability and willingness to use force is the mark of a paper tiger, and as such it cannot work in asymmetrical negotiation. With the end of the Cold War and with Moscow-Seoul normalization, the nuclear card suddenly became a very potent lever for North Korea. The DPRK has striven to use its nuclear weapons program as an all-purpose, cost-effective instrument of foreign policy. For Pyongyang, the nuclear program is a military deterrent, an equalizer in national identity competition with South Korea (which lacks nuclear weapons), a bargaining chip for extracting economic concessions from the United States and China, and a cost-effective insurance policy for regime survival. International uncertainty surrounding actual nuclear capabilities, deliberately nurtured by North Korea, has gone a long way for that small country. It is through the combination of putative military power and the on-again, off-again tit-for-tat diplomacy on the part of Pyongyang that it has gained not only the upper hand over the forces that seek to crush it, but also economic assistance from wealthy capitalist countries. All such manna has come from the abiding fear of war held by those nations that regard North Korea as an enemy.[134]

To abandon such a military posture, including its nuclear capability, would be to leave Pyongyang without the single most important lever in its asymmetric conflicts and negotiations with South Korea, the United

States, and Japan. Instead, Pyongyang follows its own third way — a maxi-mini strategy, doing the minimum necessary to get the maximum possible aid from South Korea and other countries without reducing its minimum deterrent military power.

North Korean nuclear and missile brinkmanship also illustrates with particular clarity that when the enactment of a national identity is blocked in one domain, it seeks to compensate in another. From Pyongyang's military-first perspective, developing asymmetrical capabilities such as ballistic missiles and WMD serves as strategic sine qua non in its survival strategy, as well as an equalizer in the legitimacy war and status competition with the South. It remains one of the few areas in which the DPRK commands a comparative advantage in the military balance of power with the South. North Korea's humiliating defeat by its southern counterpart in the first-ever naval clash in June 1999 further emphasizes its WMD and ballistic missiles as a strategic equalizer.

In short, Pyongyang's proximity to the strategic field of play, its high stakes, resolve, and control, its relative asymmetrical military capabilities, and its coercive leverage strategy have all combined to enable the DPRK to exercise bargaining power far disproportionate to its aggregate structural power.

That said, however, Kim Jong Il's pronounced commitment to survival strategy would not stand in the way of his demonstrating situation-specific flexibility, especially in foreign policy. Indeed, Pyongyang has pursued a great variety of coping strategies, such as brinkmanship, beggar diplomacy, tit-for-tat cooperative strategy, overseas arms sales, appeals for humanitarian aid, and on-again, off-again joint-venture projects, to generate desperately needed foreign capital.

The Quest for Development

During the long Cold War years, geopolitics and ideology combined to make it possible for Pyongyang to gain significant economic, military, and security benefits from larger socialist allies, especially Moscow and Beijing, and to claim thereby that the North Korean system was a success. In the late 1950s and much of the 1960s, the political economy of North Korea did indeed seem headed toward becoming an exceptional model of an autocentric, socialist, and self-reliant national economy afloat in the sea of the capitalist world system.

Determined not to be outperformed in the legitimation-cum-economic war, in 1972 Pyongyang launched its first international shopping expeditions for capital and technology, accumulating in a few years (1972 to 1975) a trade deficit of about $1.3 billion with non-Communist countries and $700 million with Communist countries. This was the genesis of Pyongyang's debt trap.[135] Hit by the rapidly deteriorating terms of trade (the oil crisis and declining metal prices), Pyongyang defaulted on its debts in 1975, with the dual consequences of effectively cutting itself off from Western capital markets and becoming more dependent on the Soviet Union than ever before.

The situation worsened in the late 1980s as opportunities to grow through marshaling greater resources began to dwindle and as relations began to deteriorate with the principal socialist patron, Gorbachev's Soviet Union. This forced Pyongyang to become more dependent on other socialist countries for support. The collapse of the Soviet Union and the subsequent breakup of the Eastern bloc was a major macroeconomic shock that ushered in a period of as yet unchecked decline.[136]

One of the most telling paradoxes of North Korea's political economy during the Cold War is the extent to which Pyongyang successfully managed to have its *juche* (self-reliance) cake and eat it too. As an appealing legitimating principle, *juche* often has been turned on its head to conceal a high degree of dependence on Soviet and Chinese aid. Between 1948 and 1984, Moscow and Beijing were Pyongyang's first and second most important patrons, supplying $2.2 billion and $900 million in aid, respectively.[137] Thanks to the East-West and Sino-Soviet rivalries during the Cold War, Pyongyang was allowed to practice such concealed mendicant diplomacy. The collapse of the Soviet Union was the most serious shock to socialist North Korea, not only for the cessation of aid and the virtual demise of concessional trade (dropping from 56.3 percent in 1990 to 5.3 percent in 2000), but also because it delivered a wrenching blow to the much-trumpeted *juche*-based national identity.

North Korea's economic collapse in the 1990s was the inevitable result of Pyongyang's massive expenditures on military preparedness and the demise of Soviet aid and trade. In a contradictory yet revealing manner, Pyongyang admitted as much when it attributed the failure of the Third Seven-Year Plan (1987 to 1993) to a series of adverse external shocks: the "collusion between the imperialists and counter-revolutionary forces" and the "penetration of imperialist ideology and culture" that had accelerated the demise of the Second (Socialist) World and the end of Soviet aid.[138] As much as Pyongyang may blame the economic crisis on such external shocks or on natural disaster at home, the root causes of the economic crisis are deeply systemic. The adverse external circumstances in the early 1990s and the bad weather in 1995 and 1996 served only as triggering and exacerbating factors.

The political economy of post–Kim Il Sung North Korea finds itself in a vicious circle: a successful export strategy is not possible without massive imports of high-tech equipment and plants, which in turn would not be possible without hard-currency credits, which in turn would not be possible without first paying off its foreign debts through a successful export strategy, and so on. The defining features of North Korea's external economic relations in the post–Cold War era include: (1) the extreme degree to which markets were repressed, with the resulting shrinkage of foreign trade; (2) a chronic trade deficit; (3) a lack of access to international capital markets due to the 1975 debt default; and (4) a highly unusual balance-of-payments profile that must be financed in highly unconventional ways.[139]

As shown in Tables 6 and 7, Northeast Asia figures most prominently in North Korea's foreign trade, with China (40 percent), South Korea (26 percent), Russia (6 percent), and Japan (4.8 percent), in that order, accounting for more than 77 percent of Pyongyang's total global trade in 2005. The first 5 years of the new millennium (2001–05) have brought about significant changes in the pattern and volume of North Korea's foreign trade. While total volume increased by 52 percent (from $2.67 billion in 2001 to $4.0 billion in 2005), China's and South Korea's shares increased by 114 percent (from $737.5 million to $1,580 million) and 162 percent (from $403 million to $1,055 million), respectively. Japan's share declined from 17.8 percent to 4.8 percent ($475 million to $195 million), while Russia's share increased from 2.6 percent to 6.0 percent ($68.3 million to $213.4 million).

Seen in this light, Chinese-style reform and opening are widely believed to be the most promising way out of the poverty trap. Post-Mao China's record doubling of per capita output in the shortest period (1977-87)[140]

Year	Export Volume	Export Growth Rate (%)	Import Volume	Import Growth Rate (%)	Total Volume	Total Growth Rate (%)
1990	1,733	-	2,437	-	4,170	-
1991	945	-45.5	1,639	-32.7	2,584	-38.0
1992	933	-1.3	1,622	-1.0	2,555	-1.1
1993	990	6.1	1,656	2.1	2,646	3.6
1994	858	-13.3	1,242	-25.0	2,100	-20.6
1995	736	-14.2	1,316	6.0	2,052	-2.3
1996	726	-1.4	1,250	-5.0	1,976	-3.7
1997	904	24.5	1,272	1.8	2,177	10.2
1998	559	-38.2	883	-30.6	1,442	-33.8
1999	515	-7.9	965	9.3	1,480	2.6
2000	556	8.0	1,413	46.4	1,970	33.1
2001	650	16.9	1,620	14.6	2,270	15.2
2002	735	13.1	1,525	-5.9	2,260	-0.4
2003	777	5.7	1,614	5.8	2,391	5.8
2004	1,020	31.3	1,837	13.8	2,857	19.5
2005					3,000	5.0

Sources: ROK Ministry of Unification and Korean Trade Association (KOTRA).

Table 6. North Korea's Foreign Trade (Excluding North-South Trade), 1990-2005 (Unit: U.S.$ million).

Country	2001 Trade Volume	2001 Share (%)	2002 Trade Volume	2002 Share (%)	2003 Trade Volume	2003 Share (%)	2004 Trade Volume	2004 Share (%)	2005 Trade Volume	2005 Share (%)
China	737.5	27.6%	738.0	25.4%	1,022.9	32.8%	1,385.2	39.0%	1,580.3	39.0%
South Korea	403.0	15.1%	641.7	22.1%	724.2	23.2%	697.0	19.6%	1,055	26.0%
Thailand	130	4.9%	216.6	7.5%	254.3	8.2%	329.9	9.3%	329	8.1%
Japan	474.7	17.8%	369.5	12.7%	265.3	8.5%	252.6	7.1%	195	4.8%
Russia	68.3	2.6%	80.7	2.8%	118.4	3.8%	213.4	6.0%	232	5.7%
India	157.8	5.9%	191.7	6.6%	158.4	5.1%	135.0	3.8%		
Others	702.1	26.3%	663.9	22.9%	572.0	18.4%	541.0	15.2%		
Total	2,673.5	100%	2,902.1	100%	3,115.5	100%	3,554.1	100%	4,055	100%

Sources: KOTRA and ROK Ministry of Unification.

Table 7. North Korea's Top Trading Partners (Including North-South Trade) (Unit: U.S.$ million).

should serve as inspiration to North Korea to follow this path. Yet Pyongyang has issued mixed and contradictory signals and statements about post-Mao Chinese socialism. In six informal summit meetings between 1978 and 1991, Deng Xiaoping repeatedly urged Kim Il Sung to develop the economy through reform and opening. This only provoked Kim Il Sung's testy retort, "We opened, already," in reference to the Rajin-Sonbong Free Economic and Trade Zone.[141] In September 1993, however, Kim Il Sung reportedly told a visiting Chinese delegation that he admired China "for having achieved brilliant reforms and openness" while continuing to build "socialism with Chinese characteristics." He also stated that the Chinese experience would become "an encouraging factor for us Koreans."[142] In a May 1999 meeting with Chinese Ambassador Wan Yongxiang in Pyongyang, Kim Jong Il is reported to have said that he supported Chinese-style reforms. In return, he asked Beijing to respect "Korean-style socialism."[143]

The North Korean government admitted in January 2001 the need for "new thinking" to adjust ideological perspectives and work ethics to promote the "state competitiveness" required in the new century.[144] This admission was accompanied by Kim Jong Il's second "secret" visit to Shanghai in less than 8 months (January 15–20, 2001) for an extensive personal inspection of "capitalism with Shanghai characteristics." These developments prompted a flurry of wild speculation about *juche* being Shanghaied and North Korea becoming a "second China."

Despite North Korea's seeming determination to undertake economic reform and the popular perception that Chinese-style reform and opening are the most promising way, there are at least five major obstacles.

First, China's reform and opening came about during the heyday of the revived Cold War when anti-Soviet China enjoyed and exercised its maximum realpolitik leverage, as was made evident, for instance, in Beijing's easy entry into the World Bank and IMF in May 1980. Second, China's economic reforms were tied to a political changing of the guard: the ascendancy of Deng Xiaoping as the new paramount leader in December 1978 with the purging of the Gang of Four and Mao's designated heir-apparent Huo Guofeng. Despite much speculation to the contrary, Kim Jong Il seems firmly positioned to remain in power and even to name his successor in the Kim dynasty. Third, unlike post-Mao China, North Korea does not have rich, famous, and enterprising overseas Koreans to generate the level of foreign direct investment that China attracted in the 1980s. Fourth, the agriculture-led reform process we have seen in East Asian transitional economies simply may not be available to North Korea, due to the very different initial conditions that resemble East European economies or the former Soviet Union more than China or Vietnam.

The fifth obstacle has to do with Pyongyang's Catch-22 identity dilemma. To save the *juche* system would require destroying important parts of it and also would require considerable opening to and help from its capitalist southern rival. Yet to depart from the ideological continuity of the system that the Great Leader Kim Il Sung ("the father of the nation") created, developed, and passed onto the son is viewed not as a survival necessity but as an ultimate betrayal of *raison d'état*.

Nonetheless, there has been some evidence of North Korea's movement toward a system reform strategy. In 1991 the DPRK established the Rajin-Sonbong Free

Economic and Trade Zone, which has since become the Rajin-Sonbong Free Economic Zone.[145] Pyongyang also agreed to participate in the TRADP, and recently created the Sinuiju Special Autonomous Region (SAR) on the Chinese border and also the Kaesong Industrial Complex for cooperating with South Korea. Between 1992 and 2000, the DPRK wrote 47 new laws on foreign investment, and a September 1998 constitutional revision mentions "private property," "material incentives," and "cost, price, and profit" in a document that otherwise reads like an orthodox manifestation of the DPRK's *juche* philosophy.[146] During his visit to Shanghai in January 2001, Kim Jong Il highly praised the Chinese developmental model of reform and opening (with Shanghai characteristics).

On July 1, 2002, North Korea enacted a set of major economic reform measures — known as "7.1 Measures" — with the main emphasis on marketization, monetarization, decentralization, and acquisition of FDI. Specifically, the DPRK adjusted its system of controlled prices, devalued the won, raised wages, adjusted the rationing system, opened a "socialist goods trading market," gave farmers a type of property right regarding the cultivation of particular parcels of land, and extended laws for special economic zones.[147]

More recently, against the backdrop of growing containment and encirclement sanctions by Washington and Tokyo, Pyongyang has found a new pair of patrons in South Korea and China, beefing up its system-reforming developmental strategy with North Korean characteristics. South Korea surged ahead of Japan as North Korea's second largest trade partner in 2002 and inter-Korean trade hit an all-time high of over $1 billion in 2005. South Korea's aid in various forms (rice, fertilizer, tourism, and direct investment in the

Kaesong Industrial Complex) is now estimated to be about $1 billion, which is six times the level of 2000.[148]

Kim Jong Il's fourth state visit to China from January 10 to 18, 2006, coming on the heels of President Hu Jintao's state visit to North Korea in October 2005, culminated a series of regular bilateral exchanges of visitations and interactions between Chairman Kim Jong Il and top Chinese leaders since 2000. These exchanges emphasized their shared concerns and determination to reconstruct and renormalize the relationship on a more solid and stable footing. Even though this was an unofficial (secret) state visit, Kim Jong Il received the red carpet treatment. All nine members of the Politburo Standing Committee of the Chinese Communist Party, the most powerful political organ of the Chinese system, were mobilized to welcome Kim Jong Il in a manner on par with the greeting a U.S. president would get. In effect, Beijing was showcasing to the outside world, especially the United States, its commitment to underwriting near abroad (North Korean) stability in order to safeguard the conditions for establishing a well-off society at home.

By shifting gears from aid to a deeper system of trade and investment, China also is coaxing North Korea to follow the post-Mao Chinese style of reform and opening. In a short span of 5 years, China's trade with North Korea jumped by a factor of 3.2, from $488 million in 2001 to $1.58 billion in 2005. Over 120 Chinese companies are reported to have moved to North Korea to engage in joint ventures in a bicycle factory, in the coal and natural resources sectors, and in plans to build transportation networks, including a new highway from Hunchun to Rajin.

As if to demonstrate a tit-for-tat cooperative strategy, Kim Jong Il and his entourage (with no military officers) visited six Chinese cities (Guangzhou, Shenzhen, Zhuhai, Wuhan, Yichang, and Beijing) in 8 days, with a heavy emphasis on visits to industrial, agricultural, and educational facilities. For the record, and in terms warmer than during previous visits, Kim Jong Il is reported to have "provided expressive compliments to his hosts on the economic progress accomplished over little short of three decades" and declared that he had "trouble sleeping at night" during his visit because he was "pondering how to apply reforms to North Korea to generate the results he witnessed in Guangzhou." In his official toast offering thanks to Hu Jintao for arranging the visit, Kim said that he was "deeply impressed" by China's "shining achievements" and "exuberant development," especially China's high-tech sector.[149]

In the final analysis, any successful medium- and long-term coping strategy must be systemic, involving the institutional design and implementation of measures that are consistent and congruent across different and traditionally disparate areas of policymaking and also between domestic and foreign policies. While piecemeal tactical adaptations can yield some concessions and payoffs in the short run, a series of system reform measures pursued swiftly would yield both greater benefits and, perhaps, greater dangers.

CONCLUSIONS

There is something very old and very new in post-Cold War foreign relations of the DPRK, affirming the old saying, "The more things change, the more they remain the same." As in the Cold-War era, the centrality of the Big Four in North Korea's foreign policy thinking and behavior has remained unchanged. Indeed, the

Big Four serve as the most sensitive barometer of the general orientation of North Korean foreign relations as a whole. To be sure, since 2000 North Korea has launched diplomatic outreach, establishing official relations with most EU member states, plus such other countries as Australia, Brazil, Canada, and Turkey. Pyongyang also became a member of the Asean Regional Forum (ARF) in 2002, gaining a political foothold in Southeast Asia. But few of these efforts have moved much beyond diplomatic formalities, and few really have concentrated the minds of key foreign policymakers in Pyongyang.

Despite or perhaps even because of the great-power centrality, North Korea's relations with the Big Four Plus One changed dramatically in the post-Cold War era, especially since 2000. What is most striking about post-Cold War North Korean foreign policy is not the centrality of the Big Four but rather the extent to which the United States has functioned as a kind of force-multiplier for catalyzing some major changes and shifts in Pyongyang's international approach to affairs. North Korea has sought and found a new troika of life-supporting geopolitical patrons in China, South Korea, and Russia and also a new pair of life-supporting geo-economic patrons in China and South Korea, even as the dominant perception of the United States has shifted significantly from an indispensable life-support system to a mortal threat.

As if to nod to the DPRK's "tyranny of proximity," however, all three of North Korea's contiguous neighbors—China, Russia, and South Korea—strongly oppose what these countries perceive to be Washington's goal of regime change. For example, the Bush administration's original plan of forming broadest possible NEA united front against the DPRK on the nuclear issue eventually was turned on its head by Beijing's mediation diplomacy at the second session of the fourth round of Six Party talks, culminating in the September 19, 2005, *Joint Statement of Principles* — the first-ever successful outcome of the on-again, off-again multilateral dialogue of more than 2 years. China successfully mobilized "the coalition of the willing" in support of its fifth and final draft of the *Joint Statement* — especially on the provision of a peaceful nuclear program (light-water reactor) — with three in favor (China, South Korea, Russia), one opposed (the United States), and one abstaining or split in its position between the two (Japan), creating an 3 1/2 and 1 1/2 vote against the U.S. position.

China, South Korea, and Russia favor North Korea's proposal of a step-by-step denuclearization process based on simultaneous and reciprocal ("words for words" and "action for action") concessions.[150] By contrast, the Bush administration's CVID formula would require North Korea to reveal and permit "the publicly disclosed and observable disablement of all nuclear weapons/weapons components and key centrifuge parts" *before* the United States indicates what incentives would be offered in return. With the situation in Iraq continuing to be a major challenge, the United States cannot afford an armed conflict in Northeast Asia, and this fact alone increases both North Korean and Chinese bargaining leverage in trying to chart a nonviolent course through the Six Party process.

Beijing's commitment to underwrite gradual reform of North Korea as a cost-effective means of averting its collapse as well as establishing a harmonious and well-off society (*xiaokang shehui*) at home was brought into sharp relief during Kim Jong Il's fourth trip to China. Expanded life and reform support for North

Korea through direct assistance, a growing trade and investment relationship, and a trade deficit that serves as de facto aid were signs of China's determination to beef up a series of major economic reform measures initiated in the second half of 2002 rather than risk system collapse or regime change by the Bush administration. Kim Jong Il's visit also suggests that ties between the two socialist allies are becoming ever closer, both politically and economically, in tandem with the rapid deterioration of Pyongyang's relations with Washington and Tokyo. Adept at playing great powers off against each other, Kim Jong Il will no doubt use Chinese support to stimulate more aid without becoming too dependent on South Korea and as a powerful counterweight to the United States and Japan.

One thing that the collapsist school failed to realize is that Kim Il Sung's death actually may have created a more stable DPRK. Kim Jong Il's North Korea differs from that of his father, when the dream of unification involved the absorption of, not by, South Korea. As Georgy Bulychev suggests, "Kim Jong Il . . . is neither Nero nor Louis XIV—he thinks about 'après moi' and wants to keep the state in place, but he also understands that it is impossible to do this without change."[151] In this context, a change in the regime's strategic paradigm, rather than a change of the regime itself, looks more and more like the proper resolution to the broad concerns about North Korea's future.[152]

As it is easy to say with Korea—and particularly with anything involving North Korea—the future of North Korea's relations with the Big Four Plus One is unclear. Indeed, it seems more unclear now than it did in the early to mid 1990s when a broad swath of academics and policy analysts was predicting the imminent collapse of the North Korean regime and the reunification of Korea. The interplay between North Korea and the outside world is highly complex, variegated, and even confusing. What complicates our understanding of the shape of things to come in North Korea's foreign relations is that all countries involved have become moving targets on turbulent trajectories subject to competing and often contradictory pressures and forces.

That said, however, the way the outside world—especially the Big Four plus Seoul—responds to Pyongyang is keyed closely to the way North Korea responds to the outside world. North Korea's future is malleable rather than predetermined. This nondeterministic image of the future of the post–Kim Il Sung system opens up room for the outside world to use whatever leverage it might have to help North Korean leaders opt for one future scenario or another in the coming years.

A cornered and insecure North Korea is an unpredictable and even dangerous North Korea that may feel compelled to launch a preemptive strike, igniting a major armed conflagration in the Korean peninsula and beyond. For geopolitical, geo-economic, and other reasons, Beijing, Moscow, Seoul, and even Tokyo would be happier to see the peaceful coexistence of the two Korean states on the Korean peninsula than to cope with the turmoil, chaos, and probable massive exodus of refugees that system collapse would generate in its wake.

Despite the gloomy prospects for near-term movement on the negotiating front in Beijing, the Six Party process offers an opportunity to produce something larger than mere resolution of the specific issue of North Korea's nuclear program. Not only is regional and global multilateralism now an integral part of security thinking in Beijing, Moscow, Seoul, and Tokyo, it also is a useful instrument for the much needed conflict management mechanisms in Northeast Asia. Therefore we should seize the twin historical opportunities of China's rising multilateralism and the Six Party process in the interests of forming and institutionalizing a truly Northeast Asian security regime. The Northeast Asian states need to expand multilateral dialogue and economic integration in the interests of building order and solving problems. The U.S.-DPRK standoff risks derailing burgeoning Northeast Asian regionalism, yet it is this very regionalism that will help prevent future spirals like that characterizing both nuclear standoffs between the United States and North Korea.

ENDNOTES

1. See Michael Green, "North Korean Regime Crisis: US Perspectives and Responses," *Korean Journal of Defense Analysis* Vol. 9, No. 2, Winter 1997, p. 7; and "North Korean Collapse Predicted," The Associated Press, March 6, 1997.

2. For a wide array of speculations and analyses on the future of post–Kim Il Sung North Korea, see Nicholas Eberstadt, "North Korea: Reform, Muddling Through, or Collapse?" *NBR Analysis*, Vol. 4, No. 3, 1993, pp. 5-16; *idem*, "Hastening Korean Reunification," *Foreign Affairs*, Vol. 76, No. 2, March/April 1997, pp. 77-92; Kyung-Won Kim, "No Way Out: North Korea's Impending Collapse," *Harvard International Review*, Vol. 18, No. 2, Spring 1996, pp. 22-25, 71; Gavan McCormack, "Kim Country: Hard Times in North Korea," *New Left Review*, No. 198, March-April 1993, pp. 21-48; Dae-sook Suh, "The Prospects for Change in North Korea," *Korea and World Affairs*, Vol. 17, No. 1, Spring 1993, pp. 5-20; Robert Scalapino, "North Korea at a Crossroads," Essays in Public Policy No. 73, Hoover Institution, Stanford University, 1997, pp. 1-18; Jonathan D. Pollack and Chung Min Lee, *Preparing for Korean Unification: Scenarios and Implications*, Santa Monica, CA: RAND, 1999; Nicholas Eberstadt, *The End of North Korea*,

Washington, DC: The AEI Press, 1999; Marcus Noland, *Avoiding the Apocalypse: The Future of the Two Koreas*, Washington, DC: Institute for International Economics, 2000; Samuel S. Kim, "The Future of the Post-Kim Il Sung System in North Korea," Wonmo Dong, ed., *The Two Koreas and the United States*, Armonk, NY: M. E. Sharpe, pp. 32-58; Kongdan Oh and Ralph Hassig, "North Korea Between Collapse and Reform," *Asian Survey*, Vol. 39, No. 2, March/April 1999, pp. 287-309; Marcus Noland, *North Korea After Kim Jong-il*, Washington, DC: Institute for International Economics, 2004.

3. *The Korea Times,* February 1, 2000, Internet version.

4. For application of a common-security approach in the Korean case, see Samuel S. Kim, "The Two Koreas and World Order," in Young Whan Kihl, ed., *Korea and the World: Beyond the Cold War,* Boulder, CO: Westview Press, 1994, pp. 29–65, especially pp. 56–59; Mel Gurtov, "Common Security in North Korea: Quest for a New Paradigm in Inter-Korean Relations," *Asian Survey*, Vol. 42, No. 3, May/June 2002, pp. 397–418.

5. Cited in Robert A. Pastor, "The Great Powers in the Twentieth Century: From Dawn to Dusk," in Robert A. Pastor, ed., *A Century's Journey: How the Great Powers Shape the World,* New York: Basic Books, 1999, p. 7.

6. Nicholas Eberstadt and Richard J. Ellings, "Introduction," Nicholas Eberstadt and Richard J. Ellings, eds., *Korea's Future and the Great Powers*, Seattle: University of Washington Press, 2001, p. 5.

7. According to the purchasing power parity (PPP) estimates of the World Bank, which are not unproblematic, China, with a 1994 GDP just less than $3 trillion, had become the second largest economy in the world, after the United States. By 2003, China's ranking as the world's second largest economy remained the same, but its global national income (GNI)/PPP more than doubled to $6,435 billion. See *Economist*, London, January 27, 1996, p. 102; World Bank, *World Development Report 1996*, New York: Oxford University Press, 1996, p. 188; *World Development Report 2005*, New York: Oxford University Press, 2004, p. 256.

8. The common use of "East Asia" and "Northeast Asia" as one and the same had to do with the fact that Asia, in general, and East Asia, in particular, are so overwhelmingly Sinocentric. As a result, the concept of East Asia "has conventionally referred only to those states of Confucian heritage." See John Ravenhill, "A Three Block

World? The New East Asian Regionalism," *International Relations of the Asia-Pacific,* Vol. 2, No. 2, 2002, p. 174.

9. In the 2001 *Quadrennial Defense Review* Report, "Northeast Asia" and "the East Asian littoral" are defined as "critical areas" for precluding hostile domination by any other power. See United States Department of Defense, *Quadrennial Defense Review Report,* September 30, 2001, p. 2, at *www.defenselink.mil/pubs/qdr2001.pdf,* accessed January 15, 2002.

10. Edmund L. Andrews, "Shouted Down: A Political Furor Built on Many Grudges," *New York Times,* August 3, 2005, p. C1.

11. See Barry Buzan and Rosemary Foot, eds., *Does China Matter? A Reassessment,* London: Routledge; 2004; Alastair Iain Johnston, "China's International Relations: The Political and Security Dimensions," in Samuel S. Kim, ed., *The International Relations of Northeast Asia,* Lanham, MD: Rowman & Littlefield, 2004, pp. 65–100; Robert Sutter, *China's Rise in Asia: Promises and Perils,* Lanham, MD: Rowman & Littlefield, 2005; and David Shambaugh, ed., *Power Shift: China and Asia's New Dynamics,* Berkeley: University of California Press, 2005.

12. For a detailed analysis, see Samuel S. Kim, "The Making of China's Korea Policy in the Era of Reform," in David M. Lampton, ed., *The Making of Chinese Foreign and Security Policy in the Era of Reform,* Stanford, CA: Stanford University Press, 2001, pp. 371-408.

13. "U.5.-DPRK Meeting Welcomed," *Beijing Review,* May 17-23, 1993, p. 7.

14. See Andrew Scobell, *China and North Korea: From Comrades-in-Arms to Allies at Arm's Length,* Carlisle Barracks, PA: Strategic Studies Institute, U.S. Army War College, March 2004, p. 14; and David Shambaugh, "China and the Korean Peninsula: Playing for the Long Term," *Washington Quarterly,* Vol. 26, No. 2, Spring 2003, p. 55.

15. See Edward Cody, "China Tries to Advance N. Korea Nuclear Talks," *The Washington Post,* July 31, 2005, A23; and "China Show Off Newfound Partnership at Six-Party Talks," *The Korea Herald,* August 5, 2005.

16. For an English text of the DPRK Ministry of Foreign Affairs' statement of February 10, 2005, see KCNA, February 10, 2005, available at *www.kcna.co.jp/item/2005/200502/news0211.htm,* accessed July 3, 2005.

17. "Spokesman for DPRK Foreign Ministry on Contact between Heads of DPRK and US Delegations," Korean Central News Agency, July 10, 2005.

18. *North Korea News* 724, February 28, 1994, pp. 5–6; *The Economist*, March 26, 1994, p. 39.

19. David Shambaugh, "China and the Korean Peninsula: Playing for the Long Term," *The Washington Quarterly*, Vol. 26, No. 2, 2003, p. 46.

20. Quoted in David Lampton and Richard Daniel Ewing, *The U.S.-China Relationship Facing International Security Crises: Three Case Studies in Post-9/11 Bilateral Relations*, Washington, DC: The Nixon Center, 2004, p. 70.

21. Alvin Z. Rubinstein, "Russia's Relations with North Korea," in Stephen Blank and Alvin Rubenstein, eds., *Imperial Decline: Russia's Changing Role in Asia*, Durham, NC: Duke University Press, 1997, p. 157.

22. Nikolai Sokov, "A Russian View of the Future Korean Peninsula," in Tsuneo Akaha, ed., *The Future of North Korea*, New York: Routledge, 2002, pp. 129–46.

23. Quoted in Andrew Mack, "The Nuclear Crisis on the Korean Peninsula," *Asian Survey*, Vol. 33, No. 4, April 1993, p. 342.

24. *Rodong Sinmun* [*Worker's Daily*], October 5, 1990, p. 2.; Andrew Lankov, "Cold War Alienates Seoul, Moscow," *The Korea Times*, September 17, 2004, available at *times.hankooki.com*.

25. Evgeny P. Bazhanov, "Korea in Russia's Post Cold War Regional Political Context," in Charles K. Armstrong, Gilbert Rozman, Samuel S. Kim, and Stephen Kotkin, eds., *Korea at the Center: Dynamics of Regionalism in Northeast Asia*, Armonk, NY: M. E. Sharpe, 2006, pp. 214–226.

26. Rubinstein, "Russia's Relations with North Korea," p. 164.

27. Celeste Wallander, "Wary of the West: Russian Security Policy at the Millennium," *Arms Control Today*, Vol. 30, No. 2, March 2000, pp. 7–12; "Russia's New Security Concept," *Arms Control Today*, Vol. 30, No. 1, January/February 2000, pp. 15–20; Philip C. Bleak, "Putin Signs New Military Doctrine, Fleshing Out New Security Concept," *Arms Control Today*, Vol. 30. No. 4, May 2000, p. 42.

28. For an English text of the Moscow Declaration, see KCNA, August 4, 2001, at *www.kcna.co.jp/contents/05.htm*.

29. Seung-ho Joo, "Russia and the Korean Peace Process," in Tae-Hwan Kwak and Seung-Ho Joo, eds., *The Korean Peace Process and the Four Powers*, Burlington, VT: Ashgate, 2003, pp. 143–170.

30. It is worth noting in this connection that no other great power can match Russia's summit diplomacy with both Koreas in the first 4 years of Putin's presidency — three summit meetings with Kim Jong Il (July 2000 in Pyongyang, August 2001 in Moscow, and August 2002 in Vladivostok) and two summit meetings with South Korean presidents Kim Dae Jung in February 2001 in Seoul and Roh Moo-hyun in September 2004 in Moscow.

31. Alexandre Mansourov, "Kim Jong Il Re-Embraces the Bear, Looking for the Morning Calm: North Korea's Policy Toward Russia Since 1994," in Byung Chul Koh, ed., *North Korea and the World: Explaining Pyongyang's Foreign Policy*, Seoul: Kyungnam University Press, 2004, pp. 239–284.

32. Quoted in Alexander Zhebin, "The Bush Doctrine, Russia, and Korea," in Mel Gurtov and Peter Van Ness, eds., *Confronting the Bush Doctrine: Critical Views from the Asia-Pacific*, New York: Routledge Curzon, 2005, p. 150.

33. Mansourov, "Kim Jong Il Re-Embraces the Bear, Looking for the Morning Calm," pp. 282-284.

34. The DPRK Report, NAPSNET, No. 20, October 1999, p. 1.

35. *Ibid.*, No. 24, p. 6.

36. Joo, "Russia and the Korean Peace Process."

37. Zhebin, "The Bush Doctrine, Russia, and Korea," p. 143.

38. Quoted in Elizabeth Wishnick, "Russia in Inter-Korean Relations," in Samuel S. Kim, ed., *Inter-Korean Relations: Problems and Prospects*, New York: Palgrave Macmillan 2004, p. 126.

39. Joo, "Russia and the Korean Peace Process."

40. Wishnick, "Russia in Inter-Korean Relations."

41. Zhebin, "The Bush Doctrine, Russia, and Korea," p. 144.

42. Peggy Falkenheim Meyer, "Russo-North Korean Relations," Paper presented at the International Council for Korean Studies Conference 2005, Arlington, VA, August 5-6, 2005.

43. Yu Bin, "China-Russia Relations: Presidential Politicking and Proactive Posturing," *Comparative Connections*, Vol. 6, No. 1, 2004, pp. 125-136, available at *www.csis.org/media/csis/pubs/0401q.pdf*.

44. *Ibid.*

45. Rubinstein, "Russia's Relations with North Korea," p. 173.

46. See David Woodruff, *Money Unmade: Barter and the Fate of Russian Capitalism,* Ithaca, NY: Cornell University Press, 1999.

47. For an English text of the Moscow Declaration, see KCNA, August 4, 2001; emphasis added.

48. The DPRK Report, NAPSNET, No. 26, p. 2–3. See also Elizabeth Wishnick, "Russian-North Korean Relations: A New Era?" in Samuel S. Kim and Tai Hwan Lee, eds., *North Korea and Northeast Asia,* New York: Rowman & Littlefield, pp. 139–162; Wishnick, "Russia in Inter-Korean Relations."

49. AFP, August 4, 2001.

50. Georgi Toloraya, "Korean Peninsula and Russia," *International Affairs, Moscow,* Vol. 49, No. 1, 2003, p. 28.

51. Wishnick, "Russian-North Korean Relations: A New Era?"

52. See C. S. Eliot Kang, "Japan in Inter-Korean Relations," in Samuel S. Kim, ed., *Inter-Korean Relations: Problems and Prospects,* New York: Palgrave Macmillan, 2004, pp. 99-101.

53. The rice would have come from Tokyo's own reserves of Japanese rice, which at the time was 12 times more expensive than Thai or Chinese rice. The total value amounted to 120 billion yen, more than $1 billion.

54. Victor Cha, "Japan-Korea Relations: Ending 2000 with a Whimper, Not a Bang," *Comparative Connections,* 2001, pp. 88-93, available at *www.csis.org/media/csis/pubs/0401q.pdf.*

55. Selig Harrison, "Did North Korea Cheat?" *Foreign Affairs,* Vol. 84, No. 1, 2005, pp. 99–110.

56. David Kang, "Japan: U.S. Partner or Focused on Abductees?" *The Washington Quarterly,* Vol. 28, No. 4, 2005, p. 107.

57. Hong Nack Kim, "Japanese-North Korean Relations Under the Koizumi Government," in Hong Nack Kim and Young Whan Kihl, eds., *North Korea: The Politics of Regime Survival,* Armonk, NY: M. E. Sharpe, 2006, pp. 161-182.

58. For the mercantile realism interpretation of Japan's foreign policy, see Eric Heginbotham and Richard Samuels, "Mercantile Realism and Japanese Foreign Policy," *International Security,* Vol. 22, No. 4, 1998, pp. 171–203. For a greater elaboration of the logic

of mercantile realism, see Robert Gilpin, *War and Change in World Politics*, New York: Cambridge University Press, 1981.

59. Kang, "Japan in Inter-Korean Relations."

60. For a comprehensive discussion of the 1994 nuclear crisis, see Leon Sigal, *Disarming Strangers: Nuclear Diplomacy with North Korea*, Princeton, NJ: Princeton University Press, 1998; Young Whan Kihl and Peter Hayes, *Peace and Security in Northeast Asia: The Nuclear Issue and the Korean Peninsula*, Armonk, NY: M. E. Sharpe, 1997.

61. The satellite system was billed as "multipurpose" and was not included in the official defense budget. The decision to acquire the satellites required the Japanese government to override a Diet resolution of 1969 that limited the use of space technology to nonmilitary activities. Two satellites were launched in March 2003. Kang, "Japan in Inter-Korean Relations," p. 107.

62. It has come to light recently that Japan had contemplated possible preemptive strikes against North Korean military sites in 1994. *Ibid.*, p. 107.

63. *Ibid.*, p. 108.

64. "Japan Intervention in Nuclear Issue 'Ineffective' — North Korean Radio," BBC-AAIW, January 27, 2003.

65. *The Asahi Shimbun*, April 21, 2006, available at *www.asahi. com/english/Herald-asahi/TKY200604210152.html*.

66. Japan Ministry of Foreign Affairs, *Diplomatic Bluebook, 2004*, Tokyo: Government of Japan, available at *www.mofa.go.jp/policy/ other/bluebook/2004/index.html*.

67. Tsuneo Akaha, "Japan's Policy Toward North Korea: Interests and Options," in Tsuneo Akaha, ed., *The Future of North Korea*, New York: Routledge 2002, pp. 77–94.

68. Richard Samuels, "Payback Time: Japan-North Korea Economic Relations," in Ahn Choong-yong, Nicholas Eberstadt, and Lee Young-sun, eds., *A New International Engagement Framework for North Korea? Contending Perspectives*, Washington, DC: Korean Economic Institute of America, 2004, p. 324.

69. Christopher W. Hughes, *Japan's Economic Power and Security: Japan and North Korea*, New York: Routledge, 1999, p. 133.

70. See Michael H. Armacost and Kenneth B. Pyle, "Japan and the Unification of Korea: Challenges for U.S. Policy Coordination,"

in Nicholas Eberstadt and Richard J. Ellings, eds., *Korea's Future and the Great Powers*, Seattle: University of Washington Press, 2001, p. 128.

71. Samuels, "Payback Time: Japan-North Korea Economic Relations," p. 319.

72. Christopher W. Hughes, *Japan's Economic Power and Security: Japan and North Korea* New York: Routledge, 1999, p. 132.

73. Mark E. Manyin, "Japan-North Korean Relations: Selected Issues," Washington, DC: Congressional Research Service, November 26, 2003; Samuels, "Payback Time: Japan-North Korea Economic Relations," p. 320.

74. *The Japan Times*, June 30, 2003.

75. *The Tokyo Shimbun*, November 25, 2003.

76. Xinhua News Agency, "DPRK Slashes Japan's Foreign Exchange Bill," January 31, 2004.

77. Kim, "Japanese-North Korean Relations Under the Koizumi Government."

78. Samuels, "Payback Time: Japan-North Korea Economic Relations," pp. 331-332.

79. *The Age*, Melbourne, June 25, 2003.

80. See Robert Manning, "United States-North Korean Relations: From Welfare to Workfare?" in Samuel S. Kim and Tai Hwan Lee, eds., *North Korea and Northeast Asia*, Lanham, MD: Rowman & Littlefield, 2002, pp. 61–88.

81. Testimony of Mark Minton, director of the Office of Korean Affairs, before the Senate Foreign Relations Committee, Subcommittee on East Asian and Pacific Affairs, Washington, DC, September 12, 1996.

82. Joel S. Wit, Daniel B. Poneman, and Robert L. Gallucci, *Going Critical: The First North Korean Nuclear Crisis*, Washington, DC: Brookings Institution Press, 2004, p. 27. This book, written by three American participants, easily stands out as the most authoritative and comprehensive account of the first North Korean nuclear crisis. Wit was in the State Department and Poneman with the National Security Council, while Gallucci was American chief negotiator in Geneva during the first North Korean nuclear crisis.

83. *The Pyongyang Times*, June 18, 1994, p. 2.

84. The figure of 50 to 100 nuclear weapons is Perry's extrapolation. See William J. Perry, "It's Either Nukes or Negotiation," *Washington Post,* July 23, 2003, p. A23.

85. *Rodong Sinmun* [*Worker's Daily*], December 1, 1994.

86. See "Nuclear Nonproliferation—Implications of the U.S./North Korean Agreement on Nuclear Issues," GAO Report to the Chairman, Committee on Energy and Natural Resources, U.S. Senate, October 1996, GAO/RCED/NSIAD-97-8.

87. William Perry, "Review of United States Policy Toward North Korea: Findings and Recommendations," October 12, 1999, available at *www.state.gov/www/regions/eap/991012_northkorea_rpt.html.*

88. KCNA, February 22, 2001.

89. *Ibid.*, June 18, 2001.

90. See Bruce B. Auster and Kevin Whitelaw, "Upping the Ante for Kim Jong Il: Pentagon Plan 5030, A New Blueprint for Facing Down North Korea," *U.S. News & World Report,* July 21, 2003, p. 21.

91. Jonathan D. Pollack, "The United States, North Korea, and the End of the Agreed Framework," *Naval War College Review,* Vol. 56, No. 3, 2003, pp. 11–49.

92. Quoted in David Sanger, "Intelligence Puzzle: North Korean Bombs," *New York Times,* October 14, 2003, p. A9.

93. Charles Pritchard, "A Guarantee to Bring Kim into Line," *The Financial Times,* October 10, 2003.

94. Public Broadcast Service interview, Washington, DC, September 17, 1999, as provided by NAPSNet, September 30, 1999, available at *www.nautilus.org/napsnet/dr/9909/Sep20.html#item4.*

95. KCNA, August 29, 2003.

96. "Bush's Hard Line with North Korea," *New York Times,* February 14, 2002.

97. CBS News, "Powell: U.S.—N. Korea Nuclear Deal Dead," October 20, 2002, available at *www.cbsnews.com/stories/2002/10/21/world/main526243.shtml.*

98. See KCNA, "Conclusion of Nonaggression Treaty between DPRK and U.S. Called For," October 25, 2002, available at *www.kcna.co.jp/item/2002/200210/news10/25.htm,* accessed November 22, 2005. See also Michael O'Hanlon and Mike Mochizuki, *Crisis on*

the Korean Peninsula: How to Deal with a Nuclear North Korea, New York: McGraw-Hill, 2003, for a "grand bargain" proposal from an American perspective.

99. See KCNA, "Keynote Speeches Made at Six-way Talks," August 29, 2003, available at *www.kcna.co.jp/item/2003/200308/news08/30.htm*.

100. Agence France-Presse, "US Seeks Partners for Multilateral Security Pact with North Korea," October 11, 2003.

101. KCNA, October 25, 2003, available at *www.kcna.co.jp/item/2003/200310/news10/27.htm*.

102. For an English text of the DPRK Ministry of Foreign Affairs statement of February 10, 2005, see KCNA, February 10, 2005, available at *www.kcna.co.jp/item/2005/200502/news0211.htm*, accessed July 3, 2005.

103. See "N. Korea, U.S. Could Spend More Time Alone Together," *Chosun Ilbo,* July 10, 2005.

104. See Donald G. Gross, "U.S.-Korea Relations: The Six-Party Talks: What Goes Up Can Also Come Down," *Comparative Connections,* Vol. 7, No. 4, January 2006, p. 44.

105. Gavan McCormack, *Target North Korea: Pushing North Korea to the Brink of Nuclear Catastrophe*, New York: Nation Books, 2004, p. 150. For a similar analysis of U.S. nuclear hegemony in Korea, see Peter Hayes, "American Nuclear Hegemony in Korea," *Journal of Peace Research*, Vol. 25, No. 4, 1988, pp. 351–364; Jae-Jung Suh, "Imbalance of Power, Balance of Asymmetric Terror: Mutual Assured Destruction (MAD) in Korea," in John Feffer, ed., *The Future of U.S.-Korean Relations,* New York: Routledge, 2006. pp. 64-80.

106. See Nicholas Eberstadt, "U.S.-North Korea Economic Relations: Indications from North Korea's Past Trade Performance," in Tong Whan Park, ed., *The U.S. and the Two Koreas: A New Triangle,* Boulder, CO: Lynne Rienner, 1998, p. 121.

107. For a more detailed analysis, see Samuel S. Kim, ed., *Inter-Korean Relations: Problems and Prospects*, New York: Palgrave Macmillan, 2004.

108. Young Shik Yang, "Kim Dae-jung Administration's North Korea Policy," *Korea Focus,* Vol. 6, No. 6, 1998, p. 48.

109. Roland Bleiker, *Divided Korea: Toward a Culture of Reconciliation,* Minneapolis: University of Minnesota Press, 2005, p. xliii.

110. For a full English text, see Yonhap News Agency, March 9, 2000.

111. Article III(3) of the 1994 U.S.-DPRK Agreed Framework stipulates: "The DPRK will engage in North-South dialogue, as this Agreed Framework will help create an atmosphere that promotes such dialogue."

112. *Rodong Sinmun* [*Worker's Daily*], Pyongyang, June 25, 2000, p. 6, emphasis added.

113. For the theory of classical functionalism espousing a gradual "peace by pieces" welfare-oriented approach to world order, see David Mitrany, *A Working Peace System,* Chicago: Quadrangle Books, 1966 [originally published in 1943 as a pamphlet].

114. Chung-in Moon, "Sustaining Inter-Korean Reconciliation: North-South Korea Cooperation," *Joint U.S.-Korea Academic Studies*, Vol. 12, 2002, pp. 231–232.

115. See Samuel S. Kim, *The Two Koreas and the Great Powers,* New York: Cambridge University Press, 2006, Table 6.2, pp. 322-324.

116. Charles K. Armstrong, "Inter-Korean Relations: A North Korean Perspective," in *Inter-Korean Relations*, p. 40.

117. Joint New Year Editorial of *Rodong Sinmun, Joson Immingun, Chongnyong Jonwi,* "Let Us Fully Demonstrate the Dignity and Might of the DPRK Under the Great Banner of Army-based Policy," January 1, 2003 at *www.kcna.comjp/item2003/200301/news01/01.htm.*

118. For a detailed analysis, see Samuel S. Kim and Matthew S. Winters, "Inter-Korean Economic Relations," in *Inter-Korean Relations,* pp. 57-80.

119. James W. Brooke, "Quietly, North Korea Opens Markets," *New York Times,* November 19, 2003, pp. W1, W7.

120. Ministry of Unification, *Tong'il paekso 2005* [*Unification White Paper 2005*], Seoul: Ministry of Unification, February 2005.

121. See Kim and Winters, "Inter-Korean Economic Relations," pp. 72-75.

122. John Feffer, "Korea's Slow-Motion Reunification," Policy Forum Online 05-53A: June 28, 2005, available at *www.nautilus.org/fora/security/0553Feffer.html.*

123. See Andrew Mack, "Why Big Nations Lose Small Wars: The Politics of Asymmetric Conflict," *World Politics*, Vol. 27, No. 2, 1975, pp. 175–200; T. V. Paul, *Asymmetric Conflicts: War Initiation by Weaker Powers*, New York: Cambridge University Press, 1994; Thomas Christensen, "Posing Problems Without Catching Up: China's Rise and Challenges for U.S. Security Policy," *International Security*, Vol. 25, No. 4, 2001, pp. 5–40.

124. Ivan Arreguin-Toft, "How the Weak Win Wars: A Theory of Asymmetric Conflict," *International* Security, Vol. 26, No. 1, 2001, pp. 93–128.

125. Richard Ned Lebow, *Between Peace and War: The Nature of International Crisis*, Baltimore: The Johns Hopkins University Press, 1981, pp. 57–97.

126. William Habeeb argues that "issue-specific structural power is the most critical component of power in asymmetrical negotiation." William Habeeb, *Power and Tactics in International Negotiation: How Weak Nations Bargain with Strong Nations*, Baltimore: Johns Hopkins University Press, 1988, pp. 21, 130.

127. Pastor, "The Great Powers in the Twentieth Century," p. 27.

128. Ronald P. Barston, "The External Relations of Small States," in August Schou and Arne Olav Brundtland, eds., *Small States in International Relations*, Stockholm: Almqvist and Wiskell, 1971, p. 46; and Habeeb, *Power and Tactics in International Negotiation*, pp. 130–131.

129. Peter Hayes, *Pacific Powderkeg: American Nuclear Dilemmas in Korea*, Lexington, MA: Lexington Books, 1991, p. xiv.

130. A 1995 RAND Corporation study concluded that there existed a "medium likelihood" of North Korea launching an attack against South Korea out of desperation. In such a case, there would be a "high likelihood" of the use of chemical weapons by the North. *New York Times*, January 28, 1996, p. 10.

131. Scott Snyder, "North Korea's Challenge of Regime Survival: Internal Problems and Implications for the Future," *Pacific Affairs*, Vol. 73, No. 4, Winter 2000/2001, p. 522.

132. President Roh's Address at the 53rd Commencement and Commissioning Ceremony of the Korea Air Force Academy, March 8, 2005, available at *english.president.go,kr/warp/app/en_ speeches/view?group_id=en_ar...*

133. Ashton B. Carter and William J. Perry, *Preventive Defense: A New Security Strategy for America*, Washington, DC: Brookings Institution Press, 1999, pp. 123–124. A footnote for this statement explains that Ashton Carter was not present for the meeting referred to here, so Perry "tells this story himself," p. 123.

134. *Rodong Sinmun*, June 1, 2000, p. 6.

135. Byung Chul Koh, *The Foreign Policy Systems of North and South Korea*, Berkeley: University of California Press, 1984, pp. 42–43.

136. Marcus Noland, *Avoiding the Apocalypse: The Future of the Two Koreas*, Washington, DC: Institute for International Economics, 2000, pp. 3-4.

137. Eui-gak Hwang, *The Korean Economies*, Oxford: Clarendon Press, 1993, Table 5.4.

138. See *Rodong Sinmun* [*Workers' Daily*], Pyongyang, May 27, 1991; February 4, 1992; October 10, 1993; and March 4, 1993.

139. See Marcus Noland, "North Korea's External Economic Relations: Globalization in 'Our Own Style'," in Samuel S. Kim and Tai Hwan Lee, eds., *North Korea and Northeast Asia*, Lanham, MD: Rowman & Littlefield, 2002, pp. 165–193.

140. World Bank, *World Development Report 1991: The Challenge of Development*, New York: Oxford University Press, 1991, p. 12, Figure 1.1.

141. Economist Intelligence Unit (EIU) *Country Report: South Korea and North Korea*, 1st Quarter, 1999, p. 40.

142. *North Korean News*, No. 702, September 27, 1993, p. 5.

143. AFP, July 16, 1999.

144. See "21 *seki nun koch'anghan chonpyon ui seki, ch'angcho ui seki ita*" ("The Twenty-First Century Is a Century of Great Change and Great Creation"), *Rodong Sinmun* [*Worker's Daily*], January 4, 2001, p. 2; "*Motun muncherul saeroun kwanchom kwa noppieso poko pulo nakacha*" ("Let Us See and Solve All Problems from a New Viewpoint and a New Height"), editorial, *Rodong Sinmun* [*Worker's Daily*], January 9, 2001, p. 1.

145. James Cotton, "The Rajin-Sonbong Free Trade Zone Experiment: North Korea in Pursuit of New International Linkage," in Samuel S. Kim, ed., *North Korean Foreign Relations in the Post-Cold War Era*, New York: Oxford University Press, 1998, pp. 212–234.

146. See Marcus Noland, "Economic Strategies for Reunification," in Nicholas Eberstadt and Richard J. Ellings, eds., *Korea's Future and the Great Powers*, Seattle: The National Bureau of Asian Research and University of Washington Press, 2001, pp. 191–228.

147. See Marcus Noland, "Famine and Reform in North Korea," Institute for International Economics Working Paper, WP 03–5, July 2003.

148. Meredith Jung-en Woo, "North Korea in 2005: Maximizing Profit to Save Socialism," *Asian Survey*, Vol. 46, No. 1, January/February 2006, pp. 51-52.

149. Scott Snyder, "China-Korea Relations: Kim Jong-il Pays Tribute to Beijing—In His Own Way," *Comparative Connections* First Quarter, 2006, pp. 110-111.

150. It is worth noting in this connection that the September 19 Joint Statement embodied many key elements that North Korea had first proposed but China emphasized in the Chairman's Statements of the second and third rounds of talks, including most notably Principle 5. It states that "the six parties agreed to take coordinated steps to implement the aforementioned consensus in a phased manner in line with the principle of 'commitment for commitment, action for action'."

151. Georgy Bulychev, "A Long-Term Strategy for North Korea," *Japan Focus*, February 15, 2005, available at *japanfocus.org/article.asp?id=222*.

152. In a similar vein, Robert Litwak argues that it is regime intention more than regime type that is the critical indicator of a country's decision to go nuclear. See Robert Litwak, "Non-Proliferation and the Dilemmas of Regime Change," *Survival*, Vol. 45, No. 4, Winter 2003, p. 11.